Finally Free to Succeed

A Step by Step Guide to Organizing your Mary Kay Business

by

Regina Zona

1663 Liberty Drive, Suite 200
Bloomington, Indiana 47403
(800) 839-8640
www.AuthorHouse.com

First published by AuthorHouse 11/03/04

ISBN: 1-4208-0873-7 (sc)

Library of Congress Control Number: 2004098490

Printed in the United States of America
Bloomington, Indiana

This book is printed on acid-free paper.

To all the Mary Kay Directors and Consultants
who have opened their homes and their minds to me
and taught me what Go Give is all about

and to Pat
who has given me unending support
no matter what crazy ideas I come up with.

Table of Contents

Introduction

My I-Story

I'm an opera singer. I'm also a voice teacher and affiliate professor of music at a University in Connecticut. OK, now you're thinking, "Why on earth did I buy this book from a singer? What could she possibly know that could help me?" Well, fear not...I am also a Mary Kay Consultant and I founded my own company called *Organizational System Solutions*. I am a personal organizer working exclusively with Mary Kay Directors and Consultants. I have spent the last two and a half years organizing the offices and lives of several Directors and Consultants in the Connecticut, New Jersey and Long Island areas.

About three years ago, I was teaching one of my talented voice students who had just graduated from college. I had noticed that over the previous several months she had been wearing this little round gold pin to her lessons. She casually mentioned to me that she had become a Mary Kay Consultant and she was really excited about it. "Great!" I told her, although I had all the stereotypical images of the "Mary Kay Lady" dancing around in my head and was surely expecting her to rope me into a product demonstration of some kind. She never did.

Fast forward to late July...my student had to cancel her lesson one week because she was flying to Dallas for some sort of convention. Her lesson the week after she returned was fascinating. I asked her about her trip and she couldn't stop smiling and telling me what an amazing experience it was. She was so inspired. She was ready to work her way up to a management position and very soon she was going to get her free car! "Free car?" I asked. I was now mildly interested although I was certainly convinced that she drank some "juice" down in Dallas that all the cult members were required to drink for initiation. At the end of the lesson, I told her that she could bring her stuff over and do her facial thing on me. I told her I was a sucker for cosmetics and surely would buy something from her.

So I had a facial and instantly loved the Time Wise products. I purchased about $110 worth and then prodded her about this *free car* thing. She told me a little bit about it but suggested that I meet her director for coffee to get more information. I did and this Director showed me the big checks and the marketing plan and within an hour, I signed a New Consultant Agreement. I was moving from Buffalo, New York to Milford, Connecticut the very next week, didn't have a job and certainly no contacts to think of, but I did have an extra $100. Not knowing what I had gotten myself into, I anxiously awaited the arrival of my showcase.

Once I got to Connecticut, I was introduced to my soon-to-be Adoptee Director. This little spitfire had not been a Director for a full year yet, but she was a mover and a shaker with a drive for success that was quite contagious. I became inspired and motivated to achieve my dreams. I had my first skin care class and made $400! My second class was a $600 class! It was great and I was good at it. I was a Star Consultant each quarter that Seminar year, became a Star Recruiter within a few months and decided that I wanted to work toward the car.

Meanwhile, I was brand new to Connecticut and I was teaching at a University on a part time basis, but was very motivated to further my Mary Kay business. I knew that if I wanted to be successful I needed to surround myself with successful people who were achieving their dreams. So I went to my Adoptee Director (the moving and shaking spitfire) and asked her several questions about how I could move up in my Mary Kay Career. She was helpful and motivating. She also happened to mention that she needed some help in her office and she was going to hire a college student to come in a few hours a week. I asked her, "What about me? I'm excellent on the computer, I'm an organized person, and I could come in twice a week to help out." I'm no dummy. I knew that being around this woman was going to keep me motivated in my own business. She was certainly surprised at my offer, but immediately took me up on it.

In the several months that I worked for my Adoptee Director, I organized her office, put all of her paperwork on the computer, redesigned her filing system, designed a monthly newsletter, suggested a different furniture layout for efficiency, reorganized her inventory, and set up daily systems so that the office could essentially run itself very smoothly. It became a well-oiled machine as I was very independent and enthusiastic, which made it possible for her to get out of the office. While I was doing all of this for her, she was consistently giving me guidance in my Mary Kay business. We had a mutually beneficial relationship.

That year, her first full year as a Director, she was in the $400,000 Unit Club. She has always been very kind in saying that her success was due, in part, to me. Of course, this woman is a driven achiever and though she would have gotten there with or without me, I enabled her to focus on her business rather than on her office and that is one ingredient in a recipe of success.

I worked for this Director for about eight months and then I went away for a couple of months on a singing gig. I found her a suitable replacement and trained her to fill my position. I knew that I wasn't going to return to this job. I hadn't really wanted to be a full time office assistant; my interest in selling skin care and cosmetics had waned a bit and I wanted to focus on my operatic career. When I returned, I discussed this with my Adoptee Director and she understood that all I could continue to do would be to create her monthly newsletters. She suggested to me that perhaps I should market my organizational skills to other Mary Kay Directors. I could put systems into place for them that would get their offices to run as smoothly as hers did. This idea was intriguing for several reasons. First of all, organizing people's lives and offices has always been easy for me. It's something that *makes sense* in my left-brained sensibility (more about that later). Second of all, this would involve a series of short-term projects that wouldn't take up too much of my time that I could do when I wanted or needed to. And finally, I really love this company, what it stands for and how it is run, and I still wanted to be a part of it. I knew when I started my own Mary Kay business that if I were going to do anything in this company it would be to become a Director. Eventually I became uninterested in doing what it took to move up to that position, but in this job, I found that I could be a Director to the Directors!

I was on my way. I was hired by a few local Directors and then word spread like wildfire. I was getting calls from Directors all over the tri-state area. My business began to boom. I've worked with many different Directors – from brand new to NIQ - and many types of personalities – from clutter challenged to hyper-organizationally challenged. And I must say that that is the fun part of my job. I learn the personalities and habits of my clients and determine the best systems that work for those personalities. In my years of doing this, I have discovered that even though every Director is different there are certain systems that adapt very well to each type of personality. These systems are what I want to share with you.

There are many organizational books out there. There are the system specific like File Don't Pile by Pat Dorff and Leslie Deziel and Organizing for Dummies by Eileen Roth, Tami Booth (Editor), and Elizabeth Miles. There are also the overall focused living books like The 7 Habits of Highly Effective People by Stephen Covey and Coach Yourself to Success by Talane Miedaner. We shall also not forget all of the terrific documents that Mary Kay Sales Directors have created to help out their sister Directors about organizing their offices and businesses, each with something different to offer. However, what I noticed was lacking is a comprehensive guide specifically designed for the Mary Kay Director who wants to get out from under the clutter both mentally and physically and have an office that is made for an executive. It is true that we have a home-based business but there is often a difference in both attitude and altitude between a home-based business and a corporation. If you create an executive environment, you will be motivated to run your business like an executive. It is that mentality that will get you the Pink Cadillac, the Top Director Trip and the ultimate position of National Sales Director.

In this book, I have gathered all the information I could; from systems I have created myself, to several manuals including the aforementioned books, as well as ideas that I have borrowed from other Mary Kay Directors. There are ideas for every aspect of organizing your office that are specific to your Mary Kay business. However, you may find that some of these ideas are easily adaptable to other aspects of your life.

How to use this book

This book is divided into two different sections. The first section is the largest, including; the explanation of the difference between left-brain organized people and right-brained creative people, an outline of the different areas of your office and business that may need addressing, and organizational solutions for each of those areas. The second section is the action part of the book. This is where you will find the quick 10 step exercise for immediate results called *10 Things You Can Do Right Now To Get Organized* and the multi-day project called the *Seven Step Action Plan.* This intensive plan is designed to reflect what I do when a Director hires me to completely revamp her office space. You can do this program step by step all at once, or in increments, to completely reorganize your office. This plan is not for the faint of heart, but if you are committed to changing your business, the *Seven Step Action Plan* is for you.

You can use this book in many ways. While you are reading, I would suggest you have a notebook or a highlighter so you can jot down or highlight things that are interesting to you. You can read the book from cover to cover and devise a plan to get yourself organized. Or you can pick out chapters with which you know you have issues and decide to work on just that. You can skip all of the explanation and get right to the *10 Things You Can Do Right Now To Get Organized* or jump directly into the intensive *Seven Step Action Plan.* But whatever you choose to do, DO SOMETHING! You owe it to yourself to achieve your highest potential. Getting your systems in place is a major step in that process. You will be amazed at how organizing even one part of your office can change your view and clear your mind. The other great thing about it is that organization is contagious! Once you start and complete one project, you will be motivated to begin another. When your office is all done, I bet you will be in the mood to clean out your kid's rooms, your attic or garage, and your kitchen cupboards!

So let's get going!

Rightys vs. Leftys

The difference between right brainers and left brainers

I'm not talking about whether you are right handed or left handed. I'm talking about which side of your brain is more dominant. Depending on whether you are right brained or left brained, your organizational challenges differ. Here is a list of traits for each side of the brain as described by Funderstanding, an educational website.[1]

Right Brain	**Left Brain**
Random	Logical
Intuitive	Sequential
Holistic	Rational
Synthesizing	Analytical
Subjective	Objective
Looks at wholes	Looks at parts

In other words, Rightys look at the forest and Leftys see all of the trees. Rightys see the goal and start running toward it without a map. Leftys may or may not see the goal but will map out a specific plan to get there. Rightys are all about the bottom line and Leftys enjoy the details. Typically, Rightys have extremely disorganized spaces with no systems in place and Leftys will have a place to put everything. Not to say that Leftys don't ever have messy spaces; they definitely do. However, when they do deem it necessary to clean up, they have a designated spot to house all the clutter. "Getting organized" for a Righty is often an incredibly daunting task because it requires them to make decisions about little things. The details make them very uncomfortable. They know they "should" get organized but they can never find the time or desire to do it. Leftys enjoy "getting organized" because they get to spend time with their stuff; they love to find new organizational tools but often use organization as an excuse not to do their work.

I'm a Lefty and I live with a Righty. My housemate is an extreme right brainer and our differences are crystal clear. For instance, whenever I start to tell a story, I start from the very beginning and describe all the details along the way. My housemate will know exactly where I am going and she will start to finish my sentences for me. She sees the end and wants to get there. I enjoy the details (and hearing myself talk!) and try to tell the story step by step. I have since told her that she needs to just let me finish! Another example is how we clean the house. When I straighten up or clean a room, I will take everything off the surfaces, put things away in their places (even if I have to hide things in a junk drawer or closet) and essentially make everything look nice and presentable. Sometimes, I'll come home and my housemate will declare, "I cleaned the kitchen!" When I walk into the kitchen, there are still things on the counter, dishes in the sink, pots on the stove but she takes me over to the silverware drawer and opens it. It is spotless and organized. She spent an hour organizing that silverware drawer (not that it didn't need it, mind you). Her idea of organization is forcing herself to look at the details and meticulously find a solution. She finds the smallest details and tries to tackle them. This is a big task for her and this is why it is almost impossible for her to be organized in other parts of her space (like her office). She feels that the only way to get organized is to become detail-oriented, and she knows that she will never be able to keep that up for long.

Leftys have their issues too. Sometimes they "over-organize." They may have three different systems for one thing and don't commit to any of them. Sometimes they overspend on organizational tools such as folders, boxes, baskets, drawer and desk accessories, etc. to accommodate all of their many systems. Leftys also have a tendency to try to convert the Rightys. They like things their way and think that everybody's life would be easier if they would just see the light!

Perhaps I've described you or perhaps not. Some people have the perfect balance of right and left brain traits. Most lean to one side or the other. I have to say that many of the Mary Kay Directors I have come across tend to be more right brained than left brained. There is a good reason for this. Right brainers tend to be *people*-people. They are creative and have the vision of the big picture. They are excellent at sharing that vision – the vision of all the great things that Mary Kay can provide. Their enthusiasm with the "big picture" is infectious and people want to hop on board.

That is not to say that there are not wonderful and incredibly successful left brained Mary Kay Directors. They can be equally successful because they know how to break down their big goals into small steps that they follow to the top. These are the Directors that keep coming up with great new tracking sheets and production projection charts to help you stay on the right path. (Remember what I said about the Leftys needing to convert the Rightys?)

No matter what side of your brain is dominant, you can find a way to stay focused and organize your life. You just have to make the decision to do it. Have you heard that before?

Did you ever wonder if you had Attention Deficit Disorder (ADD)? You are sitting at your desk doing something and you turn your head and see something else that needs attending to. So you start that project and the first project goes uncompleted. Then when you are in the middle of that project you are distracted by yet another which then leaves the second project unfinished. This does not mean that you have a mental disorder. This means that your environment is not conducive to focused work. The organization of your space is often a reflection of how your mind is organized. This is not to say that the only way to be successful is if you have a pristinely clean office with nothing on the desk, walls or floor. But if you create a more focused environment you will create a more focused mind.

We all know that opposites attract. It is often that a Righty will end up with a Lefty because they compliment each other. However, if you tend to be the disorganized one and your partner is the organized one, you may feel put upon. Sometimes the organized partner will constantly make comments – in jest – that make you feel bad that you can't seem to get your stuff together. They may not try to convert you, they may leave you alone, but every chance they get they make a little joke about how messy your space is. However, remember that disorganization is not a character flaw. You are not a bad person doomed to mediocrity if you don't have a file system. Your partner just doesn't understand how your creative side works. All they see is clutter and most likely they have no idea what it is that you have to do to achieve your goals.

I will tell you one thing, though. Your partner will be more supportive of your business if your space doesn't look like Mary Kay threw up in it. I know that seems kind of crass, but it is true. I have spoken to husbands of Directors who have made off-the-cuff comments to me about the amount of Mary Kay "stuff" all over the place. Of course, they love their spouses, but if they haven't yet seen the monetary benefits of Mary Kay – if they only see the "stuff" - then they won't be able to see beyond that clutter.

The point is you CAN get organized! Even a right brainer can live and thrive in an organized environment because organization is not about being white glove clean. Organization is a state of mind. It is knowing that everything has a place. Organization gives you the freedom to be super-creative while still being focused on the task at hand. It is about exercising the left side of your brain so that the right side can create.

OK, am I getting a little too "motivational"?

Let's get to work!

Are you disorganized?

When we think about disorganization we generally picture a desk piled high with papers, shelves overflowing with clutter, drawers that can't shut because they are so full, and not one flat surface that is free to sit on, stand on, or place something on. That is, in fact, one form of disorganization. However, being disorganized is not just being messy and cluttered. Disorganization is a time thing, a focus thing, a mind thing. Answer these questions:

1. When you walk in your office, do you feel like your energy is drained?
2. When you spend a good deal of time in your office, do you feel less motivated?
3. When someone calls to ask you for something, can you put your finger on it immediately?
4. Do you say to yourself on a regular basis, "I need to get organized"?
5. Do you spend a lot of time reorganizing your space?
6. Do you spend a lot of money on boxes, bins, file folders, and space organizers?
7. Do you habitually buy things in bulk?
8. Do you save everything?
9. Are you ever late to appointments or events?
10. Do you wonder sometimes if you have attention deficit disorder (ADD)?
11. Does your disorganization keep you from delegating work to others?
12. Do you believe that out of sight, is out of mind?
13. Do you fill out a Weekly Plan sheet faithfully?
14. Do you successfully implement your Weekly Plans each week?
15. Do you break down your large goals into small easily achievable goals?
16. Do you achieve your goals over 90% of the time?
17. Do you feel like 24 hours is not enough in a given day?
18. Do you spend more time in your Mary Kay office than you do out in the field?

19. Do you spend more time in your Mary Kay office than you do with your family and friends?
20. Do others constantly make fun of your disorganization?

Your answers to these questions can give you a clue as to whether you have some issues with disorganization. However, this doesn't mean that you can't find a way to live your life more efficiently. And you might be surprised that it won't be that hard to make some small changes to become more organized.

What is an organized person?

Organized people are those who have balance in their life, achieve their goals, and get things done. They are the people that realize that they must have their systems in order to achieve. They are consistent and committed to those systems. They aren't necessarily obsessively neat but they don't live in clutter because they realize that clutter in their space is a reflection of clutter in their mind. Am I describing you?

First of all, and as I said before, being disorganized is not a character flaw. You are not a bad or even misguided person if your space isn't perfectly spotless and clutter-free. There are several factors that contribute to a disorganized lifestyle. Julie Morgenstern wrote a wonderful book called Organizing from the Inside Out. In this book she states that there are three basic causes of clutter. They are:

1. Technical errors – These are simple mechanical issues in your organizational systems that can be fixed quite easily.[2]
2. External realities – These are environmental issues that are beyond your control that determine how organized you can be.[3]
3. Psychological obstacles – These are the hidden obstacles from inside of you that keep you from living your life in an efficient and organized way.[4]

Ms. Morgenstern writes that once you identify these causes in yourself, you can address them and either fix them or find a way to work around them

What is disorganization costing you?

There is surely nothing wrong with you for being disorganized. However, disorganization affects every part of your life. It affects your business, your relationships, your home, and your future. Just what is it costing you? If you are disorganized:

- It costs you a promotion because you are not focused and can't realize your goals.
- It costs you friends and family because you don't have balance in your time and in your life.
- It costs you money because you continuously buy stuff to try to get yourself organized only to find out that it is inefficient.
- It costs you time because you spend more time being frustrated about being disorganized than actually working towards your goals.

I know this all seems very daunting and I'm not trying to make you feel bad at all. I want you to know that there is a way to the other side – the organized side. You just have to decide if you think you are worth it. Are you worth the effort? I think so!

So now you may be thinking, "Well, what does YOUR office look like?" My office is not always pristinely clean. I admit that freely. I will sometimes let it go for days without straightening up and a few piles will form. However, everything has its place and once a week I take the time to put everything back in its place. That is a system I have committed to and I am able to stick to it. That's really what organization is: a set of systems that you are consistent about. There are several systems laid out for you in this book which you can choose to implement or not. You can do all of them or choose just one. Either way, all you need to do is make a decision! Have you heard that before?

The personal interview

When a Director is interested in hiring me to go in and organize her, I first set up a free consultation to determine how best she can use me. In this consultation the Director shows me around her office and gives me an idea of where her biggest problem areas are. Then I sit down to interview her, in order to find out which systems that she already has in place that work well for her. This is extremely important. You need to know what's working so that you can focus your attention on what's not. In her book, Organizing from the Inside Out, Julie Morgenstern says the first step to organization is to analyze.[5] Ask yourself these questions:

1. What systems are working?
2. What systems are not working?
3. What items or tools do you use that you can't live without?
4. Why do you want to get organized?
5. What is making it hard for you to get organized?

This is essentially what I am trying to find out in our initial interview. The fact of the matter is that I could easily go into any Director's office, clear the clutter, organize the space, and put systems into place. However, if there have been certain systems that Director has been using faithfully forever and I come in and change everything, she isn't going to stick to any new systems. For example, I just recently worked with a Director who would track all of her new consultants by writing information (their first order, the date of their training, the date of their debut, etc.) on the front of a file folder in which she kept all of their agreements. She kept this file folder on her desk in a paper sorter. Now, there are other efficient systems that I could have suggested to her about how to track her new consultants, most specifically by using her computer. However, she is faithful to this file folder and is consistent about it. It works for her and it would be far less efficient to try to get her to use a different system.

This is the interview sheet that I work with and I want you to take out a piece of paper and answer these questions yourself.

1. How big is your Unit?
2. What are your goals?
3. What do you feel you need to do to achieve your goals? What does your focus need to be in order to achieve your goals?
4. Do you currently have an assistant? Is she a MK Consultant?

The next several questions address your specific systems:

5. What do you do with new Customer Profiles?
6. When do you enter your customer names in the PCP list?
7. How do you process class sales? What do you do with sales tickets?
8. How do you deal with inventory control?
9. How do you correspond with your Unit? Paper, E-mail, Phone? How often?
10. How do you prepare for your Newsletter? Who creates your Newsletter? Who copies and labels your Newsletter?
11. How do you prepare your Orientation or Pace Setters Packets? How often do you update or copy them?
12. What do you do with New Consultant Agreements?
13. How do you track new consultants?
14. How do you deal with appointment scheduling?
15. What does your Success Meeting preparation entail?
16. How do you place inventory orders? How do you know what you need?
17. Do you label your product?
18. How do you track loan, borrowed and personal use product?
19. What does your filing system consist of? How often do you file?
20. Where do you keep contact information? Rolodex? PalmPilot?
21. How do you prepare mailing labels?

Finally, the sum up questions:

22. Do you feel like you are an organized person?
23. Which of these systems work very well for you?
24. What would you like me to do for you?

The reason that I ask the first 3 questions is because it is extremely important to know what it is that you are working toward. Remember the *6 Most Important Things To Do* list? At the top of the page you write your immediate goals. Then on the splatter list, you put down all the things that you need to do that day and then you decide which of those items you can delegate. Finally you write down the 6 most important tasks that will directly affect your goal. You must remember this. As a matter of fact, my Thought For The Day in my Franklin Covey Planner today is "Success is leading your life forward according to those things that are most important to you." Apropos, don't you think?

So what are your goals? What do you need to be doing to achieve those goals? The answer to that question is the same for every Director. "I need to get out and meet new women. I need to recruit." This is when the Director realizes that she cannot do that if she is stuck in her office all day.

Now look at your answer to Number 23 (Which of these systems are working well for you?). That is a very important answer. Many times when I interview a Director, the answer to that question is "None of them!" If that is the case, great! This will be an exciting journey toward organization! If there are some systems that work very well for you, meaning that you commit to them consistently, get out a highlighter and highlight them on your paper. These systems you want to embrace and work around.

Now go through the other items and determine in ranking order the least efficient systems or lack of systems you have. Remember the 5 questions of organization analysis by Julie Morgenstern. It is now time to strategize and come up with a plan of action. Determine where you want to start and figure out how you are going to do it. Estimate how long it will take and determine what you need to complete the task. Then schedule it and jump in!

Am I going too fast for you? Don't worry. As you read on you will find things that you can tackle easily without too much uprooting. I want to tell you though, that if this is all too overwhelming for you, ask for help! And if you can't find a reliable person to help you, please consider hiring a professional to help you. You might think that you can't afford it. However, if you aren't achieving your goals and getting things done because your disorganization is getting in the way, then can you really afford NOT to hire someone?

But the most important thing that needed to be done, you've already completed! You have figured out what works for you and you have isolated the problem areas. You are well on your way to gaining control of your business!

The Art of Zoning – And you don't need a permit!

When you are organizing your office space, one of the main projects is to figure out where everything is going to go. Oftentimes the solution is to put anything wherever it fits. But when you are deciding to create an efficient office space it is extremely important that you make an organized plan of where to house all of your stuff. When you are creating a plan you want to think of your office space in terms of zones – specific separate areas that house like things together.

Think of a kitchen in a high class restaurant. There is a preparation zone, a pastry zone, a pasta zone, a meat and fish zone, a dishwashing zone, a pick up zone, etc. The kitchen is divided up this way for efficiency. If the pastry chef is preparing a tart in one area of the kitchen but every time he needs whipped cream he has to walk across the room into the refrigerated area, he is wasting time and energy. He would probably also be constantly getting in the way of his co-workers which wastes both their time and energy. When designing these big kitchens, this detail is important because efficiency in a restaurant equals money! Well, guess what...efficiency in your office results in the same thing – money!

When you are designing your zones there are several areas that you need to prepare for, such as:

- The desk/workspace zone
- The computer zone
- The office supply zone
- The inventory zone
- The skin care class zone
- The packaging zone
- The samples zone
- The books and media zone
- The prize zone
- The unit meeting zone

You may be able to figure out some other zones that you need but this list represents the major ones.

Look around your office right now. How good is your zoning? Do you have your inventory spread out in several areas of your office? Are your product bags across the room from your product? Do you have your padded envelopes in one area but your stamps and packaging tape in another area? If your printer paper is in the closet far away from your printer, it may not seem like a big deal that you have to walk across the room to get new paper when you are out, but that is energy (even a little amount) that you could spend elsewhere. Zoning is all about convenience and efficiency and it will make the "flow" of energy in your office much more effective.

Now you may be thinking, "My office is way too small to have zones. I am working out of a closet!" The fact is that it doesn't matter how big or small your office is. Zoning is possible in all spaces. Some people may zone their office supplies in an extra closet if they have that space. Some people with smaller spaces would zone their office supplies in a filing box that they store under their desk. It doesn't matter what kind of space you have; just make sure that within that space you organize everything in zones.

The desk/workspace zone

These are the items that would appear in this zone:

- Desk and chair
- Computer and printer
- Datebook
- Focus Folder and Daily Phone Journal
- Rolodex/Address book
- Small amount of usable desk supplies (pens, stapler, scissors, etc.)
- Calculator
- In/Out File System
- Personal Business Filing Drawer(s)

First, let's talk about the furniture. It is difficult for me to tell you what kind of furniture you should have in your office when everyone has different space issues. I could tell you that you must get an L-shaped desk with a hutch, but if you are that person that I mentioned above who is working out of your closet, that is a ridiculous suggestion. I will simply tell you that any desk space is fine if you are comfortable with it. I would suggest, however, that if it is possible, have your computer on a separate table other than your desk, especially if you have a standard large size monitor. Computers take up so much space and if you have no space to write or plan on your desk, you will feel very uncomfortable at your desk. If you have the room for an L-shaped desk, that is a great set up. You have room for your computer on one side and writing space on the other. If you don't have the room for a large pre-made L-shaped desk, you can make your own with your current desk and a small table or tall printer stand on one side. Or if you have the space for it, an ideal set up is to have a computer desk and a writing desk parallel to each other with your chair in between. This way you only need to be looking at the computer when you are working on it.

Also, if it is possible, your desk should have at least one supply drawer and one filing drawer. If your desk doesn't, then you will have to have a separate filing cabinet and perhaps a small plastic storage drawer that you can store on or under your desk that can house desk supplies. You can even get decorative and use those pretty hat boxes or even a shoe box if you have real space challenges.

One other very important piece of furniture that you shouldn't skimp on is a good desk chair. There are only two items that I suggest you are not cheap about - a filing cabinet and a desk chair. You spend a great deal of time sitting at your desk and you need to make sure that your chair is comfortable and provides you with proper support. Test out as many chairs as you can and get the right one for you.

Now we need to discuss the top of your desk. This is the ultimate collector, isn't it? It's a large surface that makes it so easy to throw things on. Before you know it, it is piled so high with stuff you become paralyzed by the disorganization. These are the only things (besides your computer) that should be on top of your desk at any time:

- Phone
- Datebook
- Focus Folder
- Daily Phone Journal (a spiral bound notebook with the date in the upper corner of each page that you write all of your daily notes and phone numbers)
- Rolodex (if needed)
- Small pencil cup with a few pens, letter opener and a pair of scissors
- Calculator
- Post-It® notes (if you use them)
- In/Out File System (See *The Secret to a Clutter Free Office – The In/Out File System* Chapter for information on this) - if your desk is small, this can go beside or under your desk

That's it! Are you surprised? Are you thinking that you couldn't possibly live with a desk that has those few things on it? Well, that is what a clutter-free desk is all about. Everything else – stapler, notecards, staple remover, tape, paper clips, ruler, three-hole punch, etc – belongs in a drawer. All the paper belongs in your In/Out File System, your filing cabinet or the garbage. You need to spend 10 minutes at the end of every day cleaning off the top of your desk. If you commit to that, you will soon NOT be able to live with clutter on your desk and you WILL be able to focus on your business, not your stuff.

The computer zone

Obviously the computer in the computer zone will overlap with the desk/workspace zone if your computer is on your desk. But the specific items besides the computer in this zone would include:

- Computer program disks and CDs

- Computer program manuals
- Blank disks and CDs for backup
- Printer and printer paper
- Router and external modem (if you have these items)
- Extra cables or peripherals

You only need to keep the computer program disks and manuals for your current computer and for programs you actually use. I know that seems obvious but if you have had several computers in the past, I'm sure you have accumulated many set up disks, preinstalled application disks and all the literature that goes with these computers. If you decide to give away your old computers, give the new owner all of those programs and manuals and you will be removing a great deal of clutter!

I suggest you purchase a CD portfolio to hold all of your application CDs. It is compact and easily organized. Make sure you hold on to the registration numbers which are sometimes found on the paper envelopes the CDs come in or in the inserts that are found in the CD cases. You may not have many floppy disks anymore as they are quickly becoming obsolete in favor of CDs but if you do, store them in a compact case made for floppys. The manuals can easily go on a bookshelf but remember the zoning rules! Don't put the manuals clear across the room from the CDs. Find a place where you can store all of your computer related materials in one area.

You should always have at least one ream of paper near your printer. You don't necessarily have to store all of your paper here unless you have the proper storage facility but you always want to have some paper conveniently near the printer for easy use.

The office supply zone

This zone is where you keep all of your overflow supplies. You can store all of your extra paper, tape, staples, paperclips, pens, highlighters, file folders, envelopes, and all the myriad of office supplies that you may be hoarding. You can store this zone in an extra closet or under your desk – obviously the amount of space you have will dictate the location. I really like those rolling drawer organizers (a plastic storage chest on wheels that has three or more drawers) to hold these kinds of items. They are fairly inexpensive, they stack on top of one another, and you can find them at any office supply store.

The inventory zone

Most of the Directors that I have worked with have their inventory organized very well. Why is this, do you suppose? It is because when a Director is filling an order for a customer or placing an inventory order, she knows that she has to find things easily and quickly. The amazing thing is that oftentimes she does not apply this same principle to the rest of her office!

First of all, make sure all of your inventory, the big things and the little things, are in one area. I went to one Director's office which had all of her skin care products in one corner, her glamour products in a suitcase in another corner and her fragrance and body care products clear on the other side of the room. When she or her assistant would fill an order, it was almost an aerobic activity!

Keep everything together in one area on shelving. It doesn't matter what kind of shelves you have – built-ins, stand alone, utility, armoires, wall shelves. Organize your inventory on your shelves in the same order as they appear on the regular-line order sheet. That way it is very easy to organize and you can see what you have and need. When putting your items on your shelves, leave some space for growth. If you only have 10 Time Wise Cleansers but you always want to have 20 on your shelf, make sure you leave room for the 10 extra you will buy, otherwise you will have to completely reorganize your shelves the next time you get an inventory order in. If you have very deep shelves, utilize the entire depth of the shelves by putting small items at the front of the shelf and taller items at the back.

Just make sure to keep space in between them so that you don't have a hard time differentiating between items.

I recently worked with one Director who had a fantastic system for storing her glamour items. She used a large screw/nail storage cabinet (those stand alone boxes that have several small drawers to store screws and other hardware) to house her eye and cheek colors. Each drawer was reserved for a different color which was labeled with a label maker. It was the best system I've seen for these often annoying little items. If you keep your glamour items on shelves, I strongly suggest you get those plastic organizing boxes from your local craft store (bead boxes) or from the Get Organized Company (www.getorganizedco.com). They are inexpensive and stack beautifully. Lipsticks are difficult to deal with so I strongly suggest that you purchase a storage box that allows you to store them with the ends up. This way they are very easy to see.

Some Directors and Consultants keep all of their glamour items in their suitcases which they take to classes. That is fine, although I find it a little inconvenient when you are filling orders at home and you have go through those large suitcases to find one eye color. If you have that great insulated rolling luggage that Mary Kay offered as a Star Consultant Prize a while back, they have the glamour boxes already in them. I would suggest that you store those on your shelves and slide them in your bags when you need them for a class.

You should also keep your Mary Kay plastic shopping bags in this zone so that when you need to fill an order, you simply pick up a bag and fill it in the same area. Get some of those large sticky-backed hooks and attach them to the side of your shelving unit (if that is possible). Then hang your plastic bags on those hooks and they are ready to go.

The skin care class zone

Everything you need to prepare for and take to your skin care class should be in this zone. The items that should be here are, as follows:

- GO kit (or whatever you use to run your classes)
- Face cases, trays, and facial cloths (including the extras you have that you store)
- Disposable applicators
- Inventory luggage that carries the inventory to your classes
- Windex and paper towels (or other cleaning solution to clean your face cases)

Make sure your GO kit is ready to go at all times. The easiest time to prepare your GO kit is right after a skin care class. It is fresh in your mind and saves you time when you are rushing around to get ready for your next class.

There is always the question regarding inventory that you take to classes vs. inventory you have on your shelf. Should you have inventory pre-packed at all times or does that make it difficult to fill in what is needed? How do you know what you have and need? Well, first of all it is important to remember the old adage: less is more. Do not carry your entire store with you to classes. I know that this seems obvious, but too many of us always want to be prepared for anything, so we haul everything we own to every double facial! I have mixed thoughts about pre-packing. On the one hand, it is a good idea so that when you are rushed to get to a class you can just get up and go. However, it is important that you put a system into place that addresses the issue of how to efficiently restock it.

This is what I suggest: First of all, make up a master list of everything that you want to bring to a class – how many Beauty Essential Bags you want, how many Miracle Sets, moisturizing creams, Satin Hands, etc. that you always want to have with you. Keep that list in your skin care class zone where it is easy to find. When you return from a selling appointment, after you have processed all of your sales tickets, refill your inventory bags with the products that you just sold. That way, when it is fresh in your mind, you are easily preparing for your next class. Every once in a while, check your master list and make sure everything that you want in your inventory bag is there.

The packaging zone

When I speak of packaging, I am talking about the product packaging that you use to create gifts for your customers for holidays, birthdays and other events. You want to keep everything that pertains to the creation of these delectable displays in a zone. In addition to all the supplies, you need to make sure you have the tools in this zone as well – scissors, tape, pricing tags, etc.

This is a zone that tends to get a little crazy for many Directors. Some Directors LOVE to package their inventory for every occasion. These ladies have baskets and tulle and ribbons and tissue sticking out of every drawer and crevice. I have great respect for those of you who have this talent because I lack that kind of creativity completely! However, the problem with these packaging items is that they are very difficult to store. Baskets are the worst. They don't stack easily and take up a great deal of room. The best advice I can give you is this: DON'T OVER-BUY! I know that when you go out to those bargain stores and they are selling 2500 yards of red Christmas ribbon for 25 cents, it is very hard to control yourself! But you must always ask yourself, "Do I have the room to store this?" If you are like most Directors who only package their inventory for a few major holidays a year, uncontrollable packaging supplies taking up precious space in your office is not efficient.

Another thing that I want to address is the "already packaged" items. These are packages that you've created for a holiday or event, but you didn't sell, so they sit somewhere in your office waiting a year for that holiday to roll around again. Again, the problem with these packages is that they are very difficult to store. They don't stack well and multiple items don't fit easily on shelves. The other difficulty is that the inventory items in these packages often get "lost in the system." You don't remember that they are there and by the time the holiday and event roll around again, the product is old and discontinued.

First of all, try only putting together as many packages as you think you will sell. I know that seems like a ridiculous statement because obviously you wouldn't have put them together if you didn't think they would sell! But think realistically about your past sales and try to follow your personal selling patterns. Then, if you didn't sell all that you packaged together, when the holiday or event is over, take apart the packaging and put the product back on your shelf. That way it is in front of you and you can be reminded to sell it as soon as possible.

Of course, if you want to keep a few packaged items together, that is fine. They make lovely displays to put on top of your book shelves or on a display table. But treat these items as you would treat those cute little chatchkas you have in your office. Ask yourself, "Does this inspire me? Do I love this?" If the answer to both of these questions is a resounding, "Yes!" then by all means find a lovely place to display it.

Again, I like those plastic drawer storage bins to store the packaging items in this zone. And unless you are doing this kind of packaging every month, this stuff does not need to be prominently displayed in your office. Hide it away in a closet or in another room. If you use those storage bins on wheels, it will be very simple to roll out your supplies when you need them.

Another group of items that can be considered packaging that belong in a zone are mailing supplies. Keep your packing tape, padded envelopes, return address stamp, flattened boxes and other such supplies all in one area. You can also keep your PCP free gifts near here to easily slip into packages being sent out.

The samples zone

Items in this zone include all skin care and glamour samples, Look cards and personalized MK Signature cards, as well as product postcards and mailers that you would send to your customers. I strongly suggest that you purchase sample boxes or display totes in which to keep all of those tiny, easily lost samples. And again, DON'T OVER-BUY. The sample case that MK Connections sells is wonderful and compact, but it only holds so much. Do not buy more than you can store easily.

As for postcards, first and foremost, SEND THEM OUT! I have seen piles and piles of outdated postcards in so many Directors' offices that sit there and create clutter. Make a plan to send them or drop them in the reorder bags of your customers so that they don't collect in your office. Store your postcards and Look cards in a large (6 X 9) card file and separate them by type or look. They are easily accessible that way and they tend to stay organized.

You may want to put this zone near your mailing zone so that you can easily slip samples into reorder bags.

The books and media zone

This zone deals with all of the books, tapes, CDs, and videos that you accumulate for every aspect of your business. You should put all of your business books, tapes, and CDs in one area because they are all about inspiration, training or recruiting.

Your tapes, videos, and CDs should be split up into two groups:

1) Items that you would give to your customers (product information or potential recruit media)
2) Items that you would give to your consultants or use yourself (Seminar videos, tapes of the month, etc.).

Your books should be separated into four categories:

1) Manuals (i.e., Career Essentials or Director's Manuals)
2) Business basics (i.e., John Maxwell's or Bill Cantrell's books)
3) Personal basics (i.e., Talane Miedaner's Coach Yourself to Success or THIS book!)
4) Inspiration (i.e., books on Mary Kay, Bibles, or prayer journals).

Once you've separated everything into these categories, either alphabetize them or arrange them on your shelves by size.

It is very important that you purge this area every few months or so. I will speak of this at length later, but these items have a tendency to pile up, especially if you have been in the business for many years. If you have outdated recruiting or product videos or tapes, throw them out. If you have hundreds of old tapes of the month that you know you won't listen to anymore, give them to your consultants. Also, your office is NOT the place to store The Joy of Juicing or Danielle Steele's latest steamy novel. Reserve your office only for business related items.

The prize zone

There seem to be two categories of prizes – those that you received as a Consultant or Director and those that you purchase to award to your Consultants. As far as the prizes you have earned, you need to make some decisions about them. How much do they mean to you? Are there some that are very special and others that are just trinkets? There are plaques and trophies and pins and jewelry. You need to make some decisions about those prizes. Again, ask yourself, "Does this inspire me? Do I love this?" If you can't wholeheartedly answer, "Yes," to these questions, you need to purge them. Have a special promotion for your Consultants to let go of your old prizes.

As far as the prizes you purchase to give to your Consultants, again, DON'T OVER-BUY. Jewelry and pins are not too difficult to store but when you are buying lots of purses and bags or other knick knacks, you are entering major clutter mode. If you have more Consultants win the promotion than you originally thought, you can always buy more prizes.

Make sure to have ample storage containers for your prizes. You can organize jewelry in the same kinds of boxes you store your glamour products. Those plastic storage drawers are also good for the larger items. Your unit ribbons also need to be stored in this zone and you should have a box or roll up bag to store and organize them.

The unit meeting zone

You should have all of the items you take to your unit meeting in one area, ready to go. I suggest you get a mobile hanging file box that you can take to your meetings. Make several hanging files including these categories:

- Agreements
- Announcements
- Contest Winners
- Guest List
- Handouts
- Hostess Packets
- Literature (company literature that you may want to hand out to your Consultants or guests)
- Recruiting Packets
- Training Ideas (always good to have some extra training ideas)
- Unit Meeting Planner (your notes for the meeting)
- Weekly Accomplishment Sheets Blank (to hand out)
- Weekly Accomplishment Sheets Filled (for the Summary Sheets that your Consultants hand in)

During the week as things come up, you can either throw all of your important papers, notes, winners, etc. in the *Unit Meeting* file in your In/Out File System (see the chapter about that system) and then transfer them into your Unit Meeting file box – or use this file box throughout the week to organize your papers for the meeting. You can also put folded posters, prizes and ribbons in your box so that all of your meeting supplies are in one place.

So now you have been zoned! You may come up with other zones to accommodate your office and you will probably now walk around your house and try to figure out zones for every room! Zoning is the secret to ultimate organization. So zone away!

To Purge or Not to Purge – That is the Question

It is time to talk about all that stuff. Don't be frightened! I am not going to tell you that you must throw everything out! But it is time to make some decisions. If you are dedicated to creating an efficient office space and want to stay organized, then you must only surround yourself with the things that will motivate you to work.

The hardest thing about the purging process is the fact that many people are emotionally attached to their stuff. They look at every trinket in their office and remember who gave it to them and when and why. However, considering the fact that that item was stuffed on a table underneath a pile of papers and bags, how much can it actually mean to them? If it really *means* something to you, then you should display it, giving it the respect it deserves.

The other issues are the "I might need it, just in case" or "I got a great deal on it" mentalities. I have no problem with bargain shopping – I'm a shopaholic! But if you are bringing more stuff into your space that you can store, chances are you aren't going to use all the stuff that you have bought. You will create so much clutter that stuff is going to get lost, never to be found again.

You might be someone that has all your stuff everywhere – on your desk, under your desk, in closets, under tables, on the floor, on top of shelves – everywhere! Or you might be someone who hides their clutter. At first sight, it seems like you are very organized, but then you look in corners or closets and there are piles and piles of hidden treasures! Either way, it is a necessity to rid yourself of the clutter. It does nothing but drain your energy and does not allow you the benefit of a focused and efficient working environment.

Where do I start?

My favorite way to purge is to throw everything into the middle of the room and dive in. I like this method for a couple of reasons.

First of all, it makes you "get real" because you are faced with exactly how much stuff you have and it makes you realize that you simply can't live that way anymore. Secondly, while sometimes the process seems endless, when it is finished and you have conquered that pile, the results are dramatic! I always tell my clients that, at first it will look like a tornado hit your office, but within a few hours, they will already be able to see an incredible change. Now, I am not suggesting to throw the contents of your entire office in the middle of the room, to take everything out of the closets, drawers, off of shelves, etc. all at once. You should take one area of your office, such as your desk drawers or your storage closet, and dismantle it, sort through it, and put it back together. Then move on to the next area.

Sorting, sorting and more sorting

If you have ever seen the television show *Clean Sweep* on the Home and Garden Channel, you will know exactly how I suggest you begin the purging process. I do my purging much in the same way as they do. Set up three areas (they can be an *area* if you have a large space or they can be simply a box if you have a small space). The three areas should be labeled (literally or figuratively) KEEP, TOSS, and GIVE AWAY. (I don't suggest the SELL pile that the television show uses because I realize that telling you that you must have a garage or tag sale is asking way too much!) Then you begin the **initial sort**. This is where you very quickly put things in the appropriate area or box without too much thought.

In the **Initial Sort:**

- When you pick something up and you immediately know that you don't need it, decide if you want to throw it away or give it away. Place it in the appropriate pile.
- If you can't decide what you should do with it when you pick it up immediately, put it in the KEEP pile.

- Give yourself a time limit and stick to it. The important thing about this part of the process is that it should be very fast. Set a timer for 30 minutes or 40 minutes and make sure you have completed this initial sort in this time. This is not the time to really think about what to do with the stuff. If you do, you will only get bogged down with indecision and very soon you will be too overwhelmed to complete the project.

Let's talk about the GIVE AWAY pile. There are three things you can do with the items in this pile. You can *award*, *sell*, or *donate* these items: for example, inspirational books and tapes or selling tools you can *award* to your Consultants. Run a small promotion or give out grab bag prizes at a Unit Meeting or Event. Old product or discontinued gift items you can *sell* to your customers. Make a plan to have a "Buy one, Get one Free" sale to get rid of it. Better yet, old product is the perfect item to *donate* to a woman's shelter. Make a tax deductible donation to the mission or Salvation Army or Good Will, making sure you ask for a receipt for your files.

When you have finished the **initial sort**, get rid of the TOSS and GIVE AWAY piles. Take out the trash and put the items you are giving away into your car or the garage ready to go to your car. The important thing is that you get this stuff out of your office. Just removing those things will make a world of difference to you. You will start to see progress and that is very important. We are creatures of the "quick fix" and if we don't see progress early on, we get frustrated, and sometimes get to the point of giving up. (Unfortunately, my waistline knows this fact too well!) You will also have space to begin the next step in the purging process – the **separation sort**.

In the **Separation Sort:**

- Separate the items in the KEEP pile into like piles. Put all the bags in one pile, all the chatchkas in another pile, all the books in another and so on. You are breaking your large organizational goal into smaller manageable goals so it doesn't become so overwhelming.

- Begin the process of thinking in zones by putting all like things together and deciding where they will go in your office.
- Again, give yourself a time limit for this sort. This should not take longer than the **initial sort** took.

Decision time

The final step of the purging process is the **in-depth sort**. This is when you go through the separated piles and you make hard core decisions about whether this stuff is important enough to keep.

In the **In-Depth Sort**, ask yourself these questions about every item you touch:

- Do I really need this?
- Do I LOVE this?
- Does this inspire me and motivate me to work?
- Do I have the space to store this respectfully?

If the answer to all of these questions is, "YES!" then you should keep it. If you cannot answer these questions with a resounding "YES!" then you should put them in the TOSS or GIVE AWAY pile. This is the difficult part for many people. They just can't imagine their life without their stuff. But I promise you, letting go of these objects does nothing but free you. There is a rule in business called the 80:20 rule. It states that we only use 20 percent of what we have. The other 80 percent of our stuff sits there, collecting dust. Think about it. Look in your clothes closet. If you were to take out the pieces of clothing that you wear on a regular basis, maybe every week or two, you would probably only pull out 20 percent of your closet! The other stuff sits there "for a rainy day" (or a skinny day or a fat day!). With this concept in mind, why would you hold onto those things you know in your heart have very little purpose in your office? Realize that every time you release something from your space, you are making room for something new and better to come into your life – like new consultants, commission checks, Cadillacs!

OK, now it's time to address the specific stuff that I have found in every Director's office. First, let's talk about discontinued product. I realize that you paid for it and in a perfect world, you want to sell it. But what are the chances, really, that you are going to sell that old Ravishing Red lipstick or the All the Crave set? If the product has been discontinued for over a year, you must get rid of it. As I mentioned before, a woman's shelter is a wonderful place to donate product. It gives women who can't afford cosmetics and skin care the opportunity to prepare for job interviews and such. Or, you can slip these products in reorder bags as a free "Thank you for your Order" gift. You will still get a tax deduction for these donations or gifts even if you can't get the retail price so you are not losing anything. What you are doing is gaining space on your shelves for new sellable inventory! If you really don't want to give your old product away, make a plan to sell it within the next month!

I mentioned some things in the last chapter that you can award your consultants: old tapes, CDs, inspirational books, chatchkas that you've received over the years that might inspire them, or old prizes. I had one National Sales Director-in-Qualification who had a great idea for her old Circle of Achievement plaques. She handed them to her Off-Spring Directors and instructed them to put a label with their name over hers on the plaque and display it prominently in their office. This way they had a visual aid of their goals. You can do that with any significant award that you've received that you don't have room for anymore. I know, you may be thinking, "Why on earth would I want to give away my trophies or plaques that signify my achievements in this business?" If they mean that much to you, then you should absolutely keep them. But, again, if they mean that much to you, they should be displayed prominently in a special place where they can be admired and respected. If they are thrown on a shelf amid a pile of junk, you are basically stating that they don't deserve respect. If you've been meaning to hang them up or clean off that shelf or display them in a case, promise yourself that you will do that TODAY.

Let's talk about chatchkas once and for all. I've mentioned these little gems several times all ready but they definitely deserve their own paragraph. Chatchkas are those precious little items that sit around in your office – some are decorative, some have sentimental value, some only the owner could love, but almost all of them collect dust and take up space. Now, I don't want to belittle your collections of bee covered frames, crystal roses, ceramic birds, and wooden plaques. If these things make you happy, that's wonderful. However, the problem with these items is that you tend to collect a lot of them (as gifts or prizes) and you feel obligated to display them – every one of them. Anything that you allow to take up precious space in your office must fit three criteria. It should:

- Motivate you to work.
- Inspire you to feel better about yourself
- In some way help you achieve your goals

Just like I said about your prizes, if you really love them, you should display them with respect. If you are holding on to an item just because a special person gave it to you, getting rid of it is not going to lessen the relationship you have with that person or the feelings you had when you received it. And don't get me wrong: I am not suggesting that you live in a completely sterile chatchka-free environment. I am just telling you that you need to only surround yourself with things that motivate and inspire you. Choose very carefully the items that surround you on a daily basis. They will have far more meaning to you and you won't be overwhelmed with the amount of clutter.

Are you a Bag Lady? Admit it……every Mary Kay Director is (at least in my experience). Every time you go to a company event there are endless vendors selling fabulous new bags. You are tempted and invariably give in. I admit it. I am right there with you in my love of bags. But bags are like clothes. They accumulate so much to the point of choking the life out of your space. When you get a new one, most often the old bag gets tossed in the "just in case" pile. Ninety-nine percent of the time, "just in case" never happens and that bag becomes part of your clutter. You really need to take a look at your bags and decide how many and which ones you really need. Every time I have worked with a Director, they have easily been able to purge at least 40 to 50 percent of their bags. If you haven't used it in the last three months, it can go.

Another problem area in the office is the endless pile of old office supplies. Over the years, we accumulate countless number of pens, blank address labels, binders, the latest organizational tools, and the list goes on and on. The first piece of advice I have is (and I've said this before) DON'T OVER- BUY! I will admit this, too. I love office supply stores. Hey, I'm a professional organizer! What professional organizer doesn't love office supply stores? However, if you buy things just because they would be useful, but you don't have the room to store them, you won't use them and they will simply add to the clutter. When you are out on a shopping spree, ask yourself, "Will I commit to use this in the next few days?" If so, then buy it. But then you need to make room for it in your office. That means that you must do away with your old system to implement the new one. Do you get the picture? Don't bring new things into your office until you have made space for them.

Throw away your old pens and pencils, unsharpened scissors, sheets of blank labels that only have a few labels on them, printer paper that is bent and ripped that you wouldn't want to use and recycle used printer cartridges (Office Depot has a deal where you turn in a used toner cartridge for a ream of recycled paper) – you get the picture. These items are relatively inexpensive to replace but remember the 80:20 rule. If you are only going to use 20 percent of what you have, why not have less so the 80 percent doesn't create unnecessary clutter?

Just like bags, planners and calendars are items that accumulate only to be left behind when we purchase a replacement. Donate your old planner binders if they are still good, throw them out if they are not. If you have old calendars that you are keeping because you have notes that you want to keep, go through the calendar, find the notes and transfer them to your current system. If you are still hanging on to your 1988 calendar, you might have a clutter problem. If you have tax record information in your calendars (notes taken about how far you traveled, what you spent, who you saw for lunch, etc.) keep those calendars with your yearly tax stuff. You should keep your taxes and receipts for 7 years (in case you get audited) but do not store them in your office. Put them in a safe or in a box in your attic or garage or storage closet.

One more item that tends to accumulate is Applause magazines. I suggest that you only keep, at most, the magazines for the current Seminar year. Throw the rest out. If you like some of the articles or recognition lists from earlier issues, tear them out and keep them in a file.

It is important to keep your literature current. Don't save more than one copy of outdated Look Books. You need to decide if you want to keep outdated agreements, Beauty Books, recruiting literature, and blank profile cards. Again, there are new and better replacements that are fairly inexpensive. Unless you have a plan to use your old literature within the next few weeks, throw it out and start new.

The 10-minute purge

If you know you have a lot of stuff but are not ready for a radical purge, why not start with a 10-minute purge? A 10-minute purge is a short low-committal process that you can do at anytime. Set an egg-timer for 10 minutes and stand in front of a cluttered area of your office (book or inventory shelves, desk or storage drawers, supply closet). Without moving anything out of the way, simply remove from that area the things that you can see immediately that you don't want any longer. Put them in a pile to either throw out or give away. The point is, you aren't really organizing because you shouldn't pull anything out of that area to clean it out. You are simply removing the "top layer" of stuff that you know at one glance you no longer use, need or want. If you do this once a day for a week, you will see an amazing change in your space and you are on your way to being clutter-free!

What I want you to understand is that YOU ARE NOT YOUR STUFF. The things that you hold on to do not define you. And when you make the decision to let go of these things, you are not throwing away the memories. You are creating room to bring more prosperity into your life. I am giving you permission to release and let go of the clutter that has been choking you. And when you do, you will be finally free to succeed!

Papers! Papers!
Or The Joy of Filing

Yes, it has come to the time when we must discuss filing. I know that this is probably your least favorite subject in the world. I agree with you. There is nothing very exciting about filing but it is a necessary evil. I'll try to make it a little less daunting.

There are generally four different kinds of paper pushers in my experience. Which one do you fit into?

1. **"I love my neat filing cabinet"** – these are the people that have just enough filing drawers to accommodate all their paper, there is a logical system to the file folders they have, there are no piles of paper anywhere on their desk, and they know exactly where to find any piece of paper they are looking for in a moment's notice. Let's face it – if you were this type of person, you probably don't need to read this book.
2. **"I have a filing system...sort of"** – these are the people that have a filing cabinet or several filing drawers but there is no rhyme or reason to them. There are outdated files, taxes from 10 years ago, house bills mixed in with training packets, a mixture of hanging files and manila file folders, the drawers are stuffed so full you can't put one more Post- It® into it – this is why there are still piles of paper all over, under, in, and around the desk.
3. **"Filing cabinets are a necessity"** – yes, they are, and this person has way too many of them. There are filing drawers in the desk, another filing cabinet or two in the office, and two or three filing cabinets in the garage, basement, attic, or other hidden place. However, even with all of these filing cabinets, there are still papers flying about haphazardly in the office.
4. **"What's a filing cabinet**?" – need I say more?

Most people, I have found, will fit into either #2 or #3. The fact of the matter is that there is simply too much paper in any given office, and no matter whether you have numerous filing cabinets or just one, you have to put a system in place to control it all.

I'm sure you have heard the term "paperless office." I have used it in this book. You probably think it is all a crock. "There simply can't be an office without paper." Well, to a certain degree, that is true. You will always have paper coming across your desk. However, I will teach you how to deal with much of that paper that finds itself on your desk every day in *The Secret to a Clutter Free Office - The In/Out File System* Chapter. What this chapter deals with is all the rest of it – the stored stash.

The first thing we need to do is face facts. If you look in just one of your file drawers and assess what is in there, I'm sure you can agree that you don't need 75% of it. Yes, you read that right. You don't need three-quarters of all the stuff that is in there. If you think about it, every handout, selling idea, handmade brochure, event flyer, and tracking sheet is available to you on the internet right now. Just go to Unit Net (www.UnitNet.com) or Pamela Shaw's website (www.pamelashaw.com) and you will find duplicates of what is taking up space in your filing cabinet. And let's face it. If the exact same thing is not on the internet somewhere, then there are at least 5 other new ideas that could replace it.

The other issue here is how many duplicates you have. How many times has this happened? You have a great handout that you wanted to pass out to your unit at your weekly success meeting. You wanted to make sure you had enough so you made 40 copies (even though you know you only get an average of 25 consultants at your meeting). However, only 15 unit members showed up. Now you have 25 extra copies of this great handout. Where are you going to put it? In your filing cabinet, of course. It then sits there, sight unseen, for an indeterminate amount of time. Are you nodding your head in agreement? If this were the case only for this one handout, it wouldn't be so bad, would it? However, you know that you have 10's or 100's of handouts of which you have multiple copies. If you have deemed a document important enough to keep stored in your filing cabinet, then you only need one of them. You can copy them as you need them.

The tools of a filing system

The minimum amount of filing space a Director needs is 2 or 3 file drawers. These can be built into your desk or in a separate cabinet. I suggest that if you have been a Director for over 10 years, you will have a minimum of 3 and maybe 4 filing drawers. However, here's the maximum: 1 large 4 drawer filing cabinet and 2 desk filing drawers. That's it. If you have been in the business for 15 or 20 years, I understand that you've accumulated a lot of stuff, but if you have more than 6 filing drawers full, you definitely need to downsize. Remember that almost everything you are holding on to can be found online or an excellent replacement is readily available. We'll talk about how to downsize later.

First, I want to talk about equipment. I said before that there are two items in your office that you should not be cheap about: a good desk chair and a filing cabinet. The desk chair we've already discussed. The filing cabinet, however, presents more of a challenge. There are so many cabinets out there at office supply stores or at K-Mart or Wal-Mart that are very inexpensive and match your décor and are easy to assemble. However, some of these less expensive models will actually frustrate you more than making your office an efficient space. The tell-tale signs of a cheap cabinet are, as follows: 1) the drawers don't slide open easily, and, 2) it's not weighted properly so when both drawers are open, the entire cabinet tips forward. I will promise you that if your filing cabinet has these traits, the thought of filing will frustrate you and you simply won't do it. Take your time to shop around for filing cabinets and spend your money wisely.

Also, if you are going to take the time to purge and organize your filing system, throw out all of those old folders. Invest in new crisp hanging folders and file folders. The neater your new system is, the more you will want to use it. Before you go out and purchase all new folders and supplies, start your purging process (which I will explain later). Then you will have a better idea as to how many folders you need to purchase.

Once you've decided how many you need, this is what you should buy:

- "V" bottom hanging file folders – you can choose bright colors or the totalitarian green. If you choose colors that are visually pleasing to you, you can choose to color code certain groups of files (all training files are in blue folders, all literature is in pink folders, etc.) – you should purchase these hanging file folders to fulfill 60% to 75% of your filing needs
- Box bottom hanging folders – some of your hanging folders will have sub-files in them that will be separated by manila file folders and therefore the regular "V" bottom hanging folders will be inefficient – make sure the colors of these box bottoms match your other folders and purchase these to fulfill 25% to 40% of your filing needs
- Manila (or colored) filing folders to put in the box bottom hanging folders to separate sub-categories
- Smead Viewables® hanging file folder tabs – this is an option but I will tell you, I LOVE this product. These are labels that you create with your computer and printer that get placed on a plastic tab and then protected with a clear plastic coating. You can see the title of the folder on three sides and the tab stands up over an inch above the folder making it extremely easy to read. The other great thing about this product is that the software program that creates the labels will always remember how many labels you printed so when you go to print more, it will automatically set it up to print from the last sheet of blank labels used. This means that you will never waste any unused labels. When you purchase these for the first time you need to purchase the Starter Kit which will give you 25 labels to make and the software program. This will cost about $20. After that, you will buy the refill kits which only have the labels and that runs between $6.50 and $7.00. You can purchase these at Staples or online (you can do a Google search for them). One note: unfortunately, Office Max has discontinued all Smead

products. I promise you, you will be addicted to this product once you see them!

The last thing I want to address before I talk about the purging process is the placement of your filing cabinet. If you only have file drawers in your desk, then you don't need to worry about this. However, if you have an external filing cabinet, it is very important that you don't place it too far away from your workspace. The farther it is away from you, the less likely you are to use it. Try to place it close enough to your desk so that you can easily "roll" over to it in your office chair. That way, you will not find it such an inconvenience and will be more likely to stick to your filing system. Certainly, do not have your main filing cabinet in another room. It will become a "holding cell" for your papers which will then eventually become a cemetery, never to be gone through again.

The sort and purge

OK, it's time to start tackling those filing drawers. Creating a file system is a multi-step process. These are the steps:

1. Do an **initial sort** separating things into three or four broad categories. Immediately throw out the things you know at first glance you don't need anymore.
2. Go through each big pile you initially sorted and examine every piece of paper in that pile. Throw it out or save it and if you save it, separate the papers into the categories that will make up your file system.
3. Once you've created all the file categories, put a Post-It® note on each item or group of items that is going into a file folder. Put the name of the file on that Post-It®. Alphabetize all of those items and stack them in alternating directions. Set them all aside.
4. Create your file tabs. After you put them on the file folders, put them in the appropriate drawers.

The first thing you need to do is take all the files out of the drawers and pile all of papers on, under and next to your desk in the middle of the floor. Yep, everything! You might not be able to find the floor when all is said and done, but this is a necessity. Then it is time for the **initial sort**. It is very important that during this phase, you are not spending a lot of time looking at every piece of paper you come across. Glance at it and either throw it out or put it in one of your major categories. Give yourself a time limit for this initial sort so that it forces you to get through it quickly without too much analysis at first. These are the categories that you will have for your initial sort:

- **Personal business** – this includes anything that has to do with your personal Mary Kay business – Career Car information, commission statements, MK life insurance, contacts/prospects, bank statements, etc. – anything that has to do with you and your business
- **Training** – this is anything that you would share with your consultants to teach them about the business – selling ideas, tracking sheets, Weekly Accomplishment and Plan Sheets, recruiting interview worksheets, etc.
- **Company literature** – this is anything that the company publishes that you and your consultants will use – blank agreements, Career Path brochures, Star Consultant Planner, Advance Brochure, etc.
- **Non-Mary Kay related** – this is anything else that doesn't have to do with Mary Kay – household related, family related, another business, old taxes, etc. – ideally you don't want this stuff in your MK office – if you must keep this stuff in the office make sure you have ample storage space (such as another filing drawer or cabinet) and organize these items like you are doing with your MK items – old tax returns and receipts can be stored in a safe or plastic bin and placed in your attic or basement, out of the way.

These broad categories are your future file drawers. You need to have one drawer for your personal business, one for training, and one for company literature. The only time I will suggest that you keep company literature out of a file drawer is if you have room for a literature sorter. You can purchase these at any office supply store. However, I would only use this for literature you would give to your customers or potential prospects – things like Look Books, Beauty Books, Career Path brochures, Career Car fliers, product postcards, etc. The other things like agreements, order forms, customer profiles, etc. are things that you use on a regular basis and therefore should be in your file drawer and easily accessible. Just keep your sorter neat and organized. Don't allow it to become a collector!

Once everything is separated into these large piles, it is time to get down to the nitty gritty. This is when you go through every piece of paper and decide if you want to keep it or throw it away. Ask yourself these questions:

- Will I use this in the foreseeable future (within the next month)?
- Can I find this or a suitable replacement on the internet?
- Is this important enough to take up valuable space in my filing cabinet?

Your new files

If you deem any item important enough to file make sure you keep only one copy of it and separate it from unlike items. It's also important for you to know that not every single piece of paper warrants its own file. Put like things together, for example: do not have separate files for Beauty Bash, Trash-It Sale, and "Eyes-Cream" Social. Put each of these in separate manila file folders and put all of those file folders into one hanging file called *Selling Ideas* or *Selling Events*.

Here are suggestions for the hanging files in your new file system:

Personal Business File

- Career car
- Career conference
- Challenger Newsletter
- Commission statements
- Corporate information (phone numbers, contacts, etc.)
- Director information (agreement, letters from corporate about your directorship)
- Director's Memo
- Events
- Labels
- Life insurance
- Love notes
- Newsletters (from other Directors – your newsletter information goes in your Newsletter file in the In/Out File System)
- Notes (from Director's meetings, seminar, etc.)
- Prize Catalogs – subcategories include Whitney, Oriental Trading, etc.
- Prospects
- Seminar
- Unit Analysis (from last six months)

Training File

- Booking Ideas
- Career Path
- Coaching
- Director training
- DISC Personality Training
- Gift certificates for customers
- Goal setting
- Holiday ideas
- Hostess Specials
- Image
- Inspiration/motivation
- Money management
- New consultant training
- Oaths

- Office organization
- Overcoming objections
- Pace-setters classes
- Product knowledge
- Recruiting ideas – subcategories include interview worksheets, 28 Ideas to Drive a New Car, etc.
- Scripts
- Selling ideas – subcategories include Beauty Bash, Lipstick Luncheon, Eyes Cream Social, etc.
- Surveys – subcategories include TimeWise Opinion and Career Opportunity surveys
- Time management
- Tracking sheets – subcategories include Century Club, Star Consultant tracking, 30 faces tracking, interview tracking

Company Literature File

- Advance Brochure
- Agreements (blank)
- Beauty Books
- Customer Profiles (blank)
- Discover Something More
- Look Books
- Love Legacy Leadership Booklet
- Order Sheets (including Section 2 and Director)
- Product Replacement requests
- Ready, Set, Sell Brochures
- Sales Tickets (blank)
- Seminar Awards
- Star Consultant Planner

Of course there are more files that you can have in any of these drawers but this is a good start. When you are printing out your file tab labels (Viewables®), it is also a good idea to print out a list of the labels you've created so you can have a reference as to what is in your drawers. Place all of the file tabs in the center of the file folder (5 slots from either side). This way, when you need to add more files, you don't have to change the position of all of your staggered tabs.

A side note for those of you who are computer literate and really dedicated to a completely paperless office: there is a program called PaperPort Deluxe® put out by a company named ScanSoft® that is incredible. You scan all of your documents (tax returns, pictures, receipts, documents created by other Directors, etc.) into your computer and this program organizes them into folders for you. Then it converts them into a workable file so you can change the information in the document on your computer. It's quite a powerful program that you can get at computer stores like CompUSA or online and it runs just under $100.

So congratulations! You've made it through this long and tedious chapter about filing! But I know there are still some of you that live by the rule, "Out of sight, out of mind." It is for this reason that you are convinced you can't set up and commit to a filing system like I have laid out. Well, I will say this: if that is the way you think, don't you think it is a better idea to get rid of as much paper as possible and file only the really important things? This way, anything that is filed is something that you respect and remember and can access at a moment's notice. This is the sign of a successful filing system. The choice is yours: but understand that I truly believe if you are committed to having an efficient, uncluttered and successful office space, setting up and committing to a good file system is a must.

The Secret to a Clutter Free Office – The In/Out File System

First of all, I hate stackable desk paper trays. I also hate (yes, hate) paper sorters of all kinds, big and small. You may wonder why I am so emotionally involved with these seemingly benign desktop accessories. Well, the answer is simple – these items are collectors. When you don't know what to do with a piece of paper on your desk, where do you put it? Naturally you automatically put it into a stackable tray or a paper sorter. It seems so logical and even organized to do such a thing. But what inevitably happens is that paper stays in the abyss of the paper sorter for weeks, even months and the pile gets deeper and more ominous as time goes on until you can fit nothing else in it. The frustration builds every time you try to add another measly piece of paper and it doesn't fit without effort. Then, instead of taking the time to clean out the paper tray, you start stacking papers and Post-Its® and other clutter-making items in front of, behind, or next to the paper tray. Before you know it, you are twice as cluttered as you were before you bought the desk accessory in the first place!

These items are also quite bulky and when filled with all that paper to capacity, they add to the look of clutter in the office space. Now don't get me wrong – these desk accessories are not inherently *evil*, per se. Many people use them and are faithful about cleaning them out on a regular basis. However, it has been my experience that the above scenario is the far more common one and therefore, I try to avoid them at all costs.

The system that I have developed to replace these clutter-creating desk accessories is the In/Out File System. It is compact and neat and addresses all of the paper that comes into your office. This is what you need:

- A desktop hanging file organizer – you can get these in plastic or wire mesh at your favorite office supply store
- Approximately 12 Hanging folders
- Smead Viewables® Hanging File Labeling system – this is the fantastic labeling system that I talked about in the *Papers! Papers! Or The Joy of Filing* Chapter

You should make the following file folders and put them in this order:

1. *Director* **(your name) TO DO** – put the label on the far left of the folder
2. **Assistant TO DO** – put the label on the far right of the folder
3. **Accounts Receivable** – put this label and all the rest of the labels below in the center on the file folder (5 slots from either side)
4. **Customer Sales**
5. **Customer Returns**
6. **Inventory Orders**
7. **Loan/Borrow/Personal Use**
8. **New Consultants**
9. **Newsletter**
10. **Receipts**
11. **To File**
12. **Unit Meeting**

You can add more files to this system but don't get crazy with too many. Remember, this is to keep you from being cluttered. Don't clutter the system! If there are pertinent files that you use on a regular basis for a specific period of time (i.e., a Seminar file that you need to keep out when you are planning your trip to Dallas), then take that out of your file cabinet and add it to your In/Out File System until Seminar is over and then return it to your file cabinet.

OK, now that you have set up the system, this is how you are going to use it. You will notice that most of the tasks I am about to describe are assigned to your assistant. I will discuss this at great length later but an assistant is a vital part of your success. It is that assistant who is going to keep this In/Out File System flowing *in* and more importantly, *out*. You will also notice that I refer to the Boulevard® software program a great deal in this process. I strongly believe in this program and am convinced that it is the answer to a paper free office. If you still don't use Boulevard® or another MK business software program (please strongly consider implementing this software into your business

– you won't regret it), you may adapt this In/Out file to your systems. This is how it works:

- **Director TO DO** – One thing that I consistently stress in this book is that you spend 10 minutes at the end of every single day clearing off your desk. There are always things on your desk that need your attention that you were not able to address on that day. It is those things that will go in this file on a daily basis. If you have forms to fill out, people to call, handouts to read, bills to pay, mail to open, put these things in this file until you can address them. That brings me to my next point – YOU MUST EMPTY THIS FOLDER ONCE A WEEK! Use your Weekly Plan Sheet and make sure that for about an hour or two one day a week you are consistently emptying this file. This is key. If you can't commit to this small task, your success rate at becoming completely clutter free will be lowered considerably. Schedule the file purge and follow through with each task. Don't hold things over to the next week. You will feel like you have accomplished a great thing and soon it will be a habit that you don't have to think twice about.
- **Assistant TO DO** – This is the way you will communicate with your assistant. When you have tasks that you would like completed and you think of these things when your assistant is not there, write a note and put it in this file.
- **Accounts Receivable** – In Boulevard®, when a customer owes you money, their name appears on the customer list in red. When a customer sends you the money that is owed you, the balance needs to be cleared.
    - When checks from customers come in the mail (ooh…we love those days, don't we?), take the check out of the envelope and prepare a deposit slip for your next trip to the bank.
    - Write on the envelope that the check came in, who sent it, and how much was paid.
    - Put the envelope in this file and your assistant will clear that account balance in Boulevard® and then throw out the envelope.

- **Customer Sales** – Any time you make a sale of any kind – class, facial, reorder, web order, etc. – put the customer profiles and sales tickets in this file. Your assistant will enter all of the information into Boulevard® and then throw the customer profiles and sales tickets out. Yes, they will be thrown out!
    - Skin Care Class – Gather the customer profiles and sales tickets for this class and clip them together with the hostess profile/ticket on top.
        - Be sure to mark any free or discounted gifts you have given to the hostess (or any other guest) as that needs to be reflected in Boulevard®.
        - Make sure that you mark on the sales ticket if the customer paid you so that your assistant will know.
        - Your assistant will enter the new customer into Boulevard® and create an invoice within Boulevard® to reflect the inventory that was sold.
        - This is also the time that the new customer should be added to the *My Customer* list on the Mary Kay InTouch® (www.marykayintouch.com) website. This will save time when you are enrolling your customers in the Preferred Customer Program.
    - Facial/Web Order – If this is a new customer, clip the profile to the sales ticket and your assistant will process the information in the same way as above.
    - Reorder – Make sure you write the customer's full name. Your assistant may not know who *Susie* is even though she is your best friend. On the sales ticket, make sure you mark if the customer has paid or not.

- **Customer Returns** – When a customer returns a product to you, it is important that you have a record of it for several reasons.
  1) If that product is returned to inventory that needs to be reflected into Boulevard®.
  2) If you exchanged the product for something, that also needs to be reflected in Boulevard®.
  3) If you issued a credit, that again needs to be reflected in Boulevard® so the next time that customer places an order, she will get the proper credit.

  The other important aspect of this file is to allow you to document what you would like as a replacement from the company and to make it possible for your assistant to fill out the Product Replacement Request for you. This is not the place where the product goes. Hide a little bag somewhere for the returned product and when the replacement product comes in, you can throw away the old.

  - When a customer returns a product, fill out a sales ticket with the customer's name, the product returned with a little note as to why, and what you did – issued a credit, exchanged for another product, gave her a full refund, etc.
  - Make a note at the bottom of the sales ticket what you would like as a replacement from the company (ie. Prod. Replace. Neutral Lip liner).
  - Your assistant will go to the Customer profile in Boulevard®, create an invoice for the return and then immediately process the Product Replacement Request.
  - When your assistant fills out the Product Replacement Request, they should also then create an order in Boulevard® to reflect the product that will soon be added to your inventory.
- **Inventory Orders** – You place your product orders in the Desktop Office Manager® (DOM) program, however, those orders need to also be placed in Boulevard® so

that your inventory count is always current. There are several short cuts to enter an order into Boulevard® that you should read about in the software documentation. However, if you still place your order in DOM® first, make sure you print out a copy of it and place that in this file. That way your assistant will enter the order into Boulevard® and prepare for its arrival. One short note: when you place an order, your free bonuses don't usually appear on your printouts. Handwrite them into the printed invoice so your assistant can manually enter it into the order in Boulevard®. Also use this file when you bring in new inventory that you didn't pay for (i.e., free product you received at Seminar or Career Conference). Those, too, need to be added to Boulevard®.

- **Loan/Borrow/Personal Use** – You need to get into the habit of filling out a sales ticket for each of these transactions so that they can be entered into Boulevard and your inventory can always be kept current. Put these sales tickets in this file and your assistant will process them in Boulevard®.
    - If a consultant borrows a product from you and plans to return that same product or if an exchange occurred, fill out a sales ticket with the name of the consultant, what product went out and what product came in (if any). Do the same if you borrow a product from another consultant. When the product is returned, make a note of it and put that in this file as well.
    - If the consultant purchases the product from you and the money exchanges hands immediately, create a customer in your Customer List in Boulevard® called *Suzy Consultant.* Write out a sales ticket for the product that was purchased and mark it paid. Your assistant will create an invoice for this transaction in *Suzy Consultant* just for the purpose of keeping your inventory count current. *Suzy Consultant* will never have an account balance (meaning that her name will

never appear in red in the Customer List). Only use this if the money was given when the product was delivered.

- If the consultant will pay you for the borrowed product later, then create a profile in your customer list with that Consultant's name so that when the invoice is created, it will reflect that she owes you money. You don't want to process this in the recruit list because their name will not indicate that they owe you money there.
- If you take product from your shelf for demos, personal use, or gifts write out a sales ticket and mark what the purpose is and your assistant will create an invoice for you under your name in the customer list in Boulevard®.

- **New Consultants** – This is the file where the New Consultant Agreement will go when you have a new unit member. Your assistant will then go through the appropriate steps to process your new consultant – make sure her profile is listed in Boulevard®, enter her e-mail address into your online address book, enter her address into your portable address book, etc. Then the agreement can be thrown away. Yes, I said, "It can be thrown away"! All the information is entered into your computer and will be there forever (as long as you do regular backups) and you don't need the paper. Have your assistant shred it when they are finished processing all the information so the new consultant's personal information is not vulnerable.
- **Newsletter** – You only do your newsletter once a month but in the weeks in between you will come across things that you want to include in your next publication. This is where you will put it - any flyers for upcoming events, any contest winners for recognition, any calendar items, inspirational poems that you find, sales ideas that you've received in an e-mail, etc. When your assistant is gathering all of the information for the newsletter, it's all together in that file and you don't have to scramble

to find stuff to include. That also means that this file will be emptied every month. This is NOT where you put newsletters that you receive from other Directors. Those should be in their own file in your Personal Business file drawer.

- **Receipts** – Any receipts for MK related purchases (including an invoice from your assistant for her services) should go in the file. Your assistant will process the receipts in Boulevard® as new expenses and then put the receipts in an expandable monthly tax file. Everything that goes in that tax file should be entered into Boulevard® so when tax time comes around, you don't have to sit there with a calculator and count all those little pieces of paper. You will be able to simply print out an itemized report from Boulevard® which will do all the calculations for you.
- **To File** – This file is pretty self-explanatory. When you do your 10 minute a day cleanup, there will be papers that you know need to be filed. Put those items in this file and your assistant will transfer them to your permanent filing cabinet.
- **Unit Meeting** – This file serves the same purpose as the Newsletter file in that during the week between meetings, you may come across things that you want to use in your next meeting – training ideas, handouts, recognition, events, calendar items, etc. You can store those things in this folder and empty it out when you plan your meeting. Or if you choose, you can forego this file and use your Unit Meeting file box that we discussed in *The Art of Zoning – And you don't need a permit* Chapter.

Another file you might want to include is a Weekly Accomplishment Sheet file. When your unit members turn them in, your assistant can enter all the information into Boulevard® and then ribbon them (if you do that) and put it in your Unit Meeting file for recognition.

As I said before, you can add other files to this system as you need and adapt it to your daily routines. But remember that this is an IN and OUT system, meaning this is a temporary resting place for appropriate documents. One of the main jobs of your assistant is to empty out 80% of this file system every time they come into your office.

It's pretty simple. It will take a little discipline on your part at first to adapt to this system, but once you do, you will see the fruits of your labors! Clean desk, clean office, efficient assistant, uncluttered mind, new unit members, more money, higher position, the list goes on and on!

Your Computer – Friend or Foe?

It is true. You must have a computer these days. First of all, just on a basic level, it is a way for you to keep track of your production and place orders easily. Second of all, it helps you keep in touch with your unit members and sister Directors via e-mail. But more importantly (and this is the thing you might not want to admit), the computer is a tool that can keep your office and your business running efficiently. I know that many of you are afraid to depend on this "evil machine" because you may not know a lot about it or you have been burned in the past because it crashed and you lost all of your information. This chapter will give you all the basics and hopefully some peace of mind in the use of your computer as an efficient tool that you can't live without!

Before I even get to the nitty gritty about computers, I want to make a strong recommendation: If you are still a one-computer family, you should invest in a computer specifically for you and your business. The biggest reason for this is the personal space issue. If the computer is in your office and your husband or children want to use it, they have to come into your space perhaps even when you are working and disrupt your business; frustrating to say the least. Worse yet, if the computer is not even in the office and you must leave your office to work on it, you are wasting a lot of time and energy. You need to have a sacred space to work without interruption. Seriously consider getting a second computer if this scenario describes you – they are really not that expensive anymore and will be a major tax deduction.

How much computer do you need?

Just like cars, computers become outdated the minute you "drive them off the lot." Don't fret about this. It doesn't mean you will not be able to use your computer 3 months from now without feeling like you are completely behind. The technology industry keeps improving things everyday (which is a good thing, by the way!) and therefore, within a year or so of purchasing your computer, you will find there is a bigger (or smaller which is more often the case), better and faster computer out there. This doesn't mean at all that you have to buy a new computer every year! However, when you do purchase a computer, you want to make sure it is in the top rated 10% to 15% of the computers currently on the market. This way, when the better and faster one comes out, you are not that far behind and yours may even be upgradeable.

If it has been over three years since you bought a computer, you might want to consider looking around for a new one. The technology has changed quite a bit in the last few years and many of the older computers just can't keep up. Certainly if it has been five years or more, you really want to get a new one. If you feel like you can't afford it right now, try to put it into a medium term budget. Give yourself a goal – the profit from the next 5 skin care classes you hold will all go to your new computer or you will recruit 6 new unit members and the commission from their Star orders will pay for your new computer. Whatever it is, realize that a new computer is an excellent investment especially when you are dedicated to getting yourself organized.

OK, so if you've decided that you will get a new computer sometime soon, there are some things you need to know about what to get. The first thing I want to suggest is that you buy a major brand name computer. Shop around for Gateway®, Dell®, Hewlett Packard®, Compaq® – any of those recognizable names. But, you may say, "I know this guy down the street that can put together a great computer for me for cheap". Or, that you found a great deal in an online auction or on the internet with a generic label that is right in your price range. It is not that I am pro-big corporation and I certainly don't get any kind of commission from these companies, but when you are buying a computer, you are not only buying the hardware, you are also buying customer service and technical support. If anything happens to your computer, big or small (and it will), you have to be able to rely on the company that made it to back up their product and help you to repair the problem. The companies that I mentioned are open

24 hours for technical assistance and usually, if you buy a new one, there is a 1 to 3 year warranty on that computer included in the price. As a side note, don't purchase a service contract with your new computer. It's a waste of money and you don't need it especially if the free warranty is 3 years.

As an example, I bought my Gateway® laptop a little less than 2 years ago. Just a couple of months ago I was having several weird problems with it which turned out to be a hardware problem. When I was on the phone with technical support, they deemed it too difficult to fix remotely, and asked that I send it to them for repair. In the end, they replaced my keyboard and hard drive, along with all new drivers, all of which was completely free because I have a 3 year warranty! The only thing I had to pay was $50 to ship it to them. That is the kind of service you need. If you buy from the guy down the street or from a no-name internet company, there's no guarantee that they will be around in 2 years to help you.

What is confusing about purchasing a computer is all the technical jargon – the gigahertz (GHz) and gigabytes (GB) and megabytes (MB) and USB and DRAM. Here are the basics of what you need:

- **Pentium® III or IV processor and at least 2.0 GHz**: The processor is the heart of the computer and it is what makes your computer fast or slow. Intel's Pentium® processor is the industry best. There are others out there like Celeron®, Centrino® and AMD Athlon® processors but if you can get a Pentium® IV (which is pretty standard now on new machines) you will have the most reliable processor out there. The 2.0 GHz refers to the speed – the higher number, the faster the computer - meaning that when you turn it on, or open programs, and when you are on the internet, the computer will respond quicker. A 1.1 GHz is about half as slow as a 2.0 GHz and you can now buy 3.0 GHz machines. A 2.0 GHz will do very well for you especially if you only use your computer for office and home tasks. If you want to get involved with complicated multimedia graphics and such, you need as fast a processor as you can get. However, I haven't yet met a Mary Kay Director with such a need.

- **Memory - a minimum of 256 MB but preferably 512 MB**: Memory is the temporary holding cell that your programs run in. The more memory you have the more programs you can run at one time. That means if you wanted to create a document in your word processor, check your e-mail, download music from the internet, and install a Windows® update, you can do all of those tasks simultaneously. In the old days, you would only be able to have one program open at a time. Memory is one of the most upgradeable components in your computer. You can always add more memory in the future (you have to buy a new memory card or chip) if your mother board will allow it (a mother board is where the guts of the computer all connect). However, if you get a computer that has 256 MB of memory, it will most likely be sufficient for anything you need to do in your home office, although, 512 MB ensures that you will be safe in the future without any upgrading.
- **Hard drive - at least 20 GB:** The hard drive is like the filing cabinet of the computer. This is where all of your programs and files are stored for easy access. Here's a little math lesson – generally your typical file (a document you create in your word processor) is measured in kilobytes (KB). For example, from the beginning of this chapter to right now, this document takes up 30 KB of space on the hard drive. Software programs are measured in megabytes (MB). Some software programs like Microsoft® Office are as many as 500 MB. It takes 1000 KB to make up 1 MB. It takes 1000 MB to make up 1 gigabyte (GB). That means if you have a 20 GB hard drive and have only Microsoft® Office installed on it, you've used up 2.5% of your hard drive. 20 GB is actually quite small compared to what is standard today. In fact you might not even be able to find a machine that has that small a hard drive. I just checked Gateway's® site and they are offering 40GB hard drives in their least expensive machines. Either

way, the bigger the number, the bigger the hard drive. If you plan on holding on to this computer for a while you need a decent amount of hard drive space. This concludes our math lesson for today.

- **Optical Drive - CD-RW drive is a must**: CD-RW means "Compact Disc Rewriteable". I'm sure you know what a CD Rom (which means "Compact Disc Read Only Memory") is. If you've bought a computer in the last 15 years, you have used them in your CD Rom drive. What you need to know is that CD Roms have an enormous amount of storage space – much more than an old floppy disk. A floppy disk can hold 1.1 MB of information on them and CD Roms can hold 650 MB (a small encyclopedia's worth!) but you cannot save any of your material to the CD-ROM. On the other hand, a CD-RW drive is also called a CD burner in which you can "burn" files, pictures, and even video clips onto a blank CD for storage and backup. You can even burn your own music CDs – something the kids have been doing for years! Sometimes they also offer DVD drives or DVD-RW drives which means you can burn your own DVD. This is not a necessity. You will only burn your own DVD if you are planning on making movies on your computer with your video recorder. However, a DVD drive is nice especially if you don't have DVD player in your home entertainment system. However, the only drive you really need is the CD-RW.
- **Flat screen monitor is a suggestion**: This is not a must, by any means, but if your budget allows, invest in a flat screen monitor. They take up so much less space than a traditional monitor and the picture is clear and crisp. If you are buying a laptop, a separate flat screen monitor isn't necessary.

The rest of the stuff that comes with a computer – the variety of ports (USB, serial, ps2 and parallel), video cards, PCI expansion slots – are items that you can spend money on for the "latest technology." However, the standard devices in new computers are just fine for your basic home office needs. The components detailed above are the most important.

As far as how much should you expect to pay, that depends on whether you want a desktop or a laptop. Many Directors that I meet these days are considering switching to a laptop because of its portability and because it takes up far less space in the office. However, laptops are more expensive. For the components I described above you can find a good desktop for about $700-$800. For the same components in a laptop, you can expect to spend about $1400-$1600. It all depends on your budget and how important portability is. A laptop is just as powerful as a desktop and much smaller but if you can't swing the price, investing in a good quality desktop is just as good.

You also need a good color printer and what I suggest is getting an All-in-One product. You can get a printer, fax, copier, and scanner all in one machine. It saves space and gives you options in a much less expensive way than by buying four different pieces of equipment. There are several companies that offer these – the cheapest is probably Lexmark® but there are also Hewlett Packard® and Epson®. I've seen them for as low as just over $100 but you should do a little research. I've found sometimes Lexmark® is cheap for a reason if you get my meaning. One word of caution: All-in-One machines are not meant for high volume copying. The ink cartridges are too expensive to copy 100 pages of a newsletter and you can only make a handful of copies per minute. It's much better to do your large quantity copying at a copy center and reserve your All-in-One for when you only need a few copies.

All about modems and networks

The next thing I want to talk about is modems. Even if you don't do anything else on the computer, I'm sure you've been e-mailing and checking your daily production on InTouch® (www.marykayintouch.com). That is why you have a modem. There are two main types of internet connections – dial-up and DSL or Cable. Dial-up is the older slow connection and DSL or cable is the new high speed connection. Dial-up is directly connected to your home phone line and when you want to get on the internet, your modem actually dials an access number like a phone and connects to a server. However, phone lines cannot handle a lot of information transmitting at one time and therefore, if you want to work your way around the internet on this type of connection it will often take a ridiculous amount of time to load web pages onto your screen – sometimes a full minute or more for a page that has a lot of pictures on it. Not to mention that, if you only have one phone line in your house, when you are on the internet you can't use your phone and vice versa.

DSL connections are also connected to your phone lines but in a different way, so information can be transmitted at a much faster rate and your phone service is not interrupted. Cable modems are hooked up through your TV cable connections and are a bit faster than DSL. Don't worry; it doesn't interrupt your cable service. You can watch TV and surf the net at the same time. The speed difference between a DSL/Cable modem and a dial-up modem is vast. Where it may take 45 seconds to load a page with dial-up, it will take 2 seconds with DSL or cable.

If you haven't figured it out yet, I strongly suggest that you get a high speed connection. Call your phone company to see what DSL offers they have running and do the same with the cable company. These offers change so often that I wouldn't even venture a guess as to how much you should expect to pay. However, on a monthly basis a high speed connection could cost as low as $29.95. If you are an AOL® user with your dial-up service, you are probably paying about $21.95. The extra $8 is definitely worth the upgrade! Once you've gone high speed, you'll wonder what took you so long to get it.

Another item that is extremely useful if you have multiple computers in the house is a wireless network. To set this up you need to have a wireless router and wireless adapters on your computers. A router is a little box that acts as a communication hub. You plug your high speed internet connection into it and then the wireless adapters in your computers communicate with the router to pick up the internet connection. That means that your router and high speed modem can be in your office with your desktop computer and your laptop can be in the living room without being connected to anything but you would still be able to surf the net and check your e-mail on your laptop – in the living room! Many new laptops are being built with wireless adapters in them so you would only need to get a router. If your laptop didn't come with one you just need to get an adapter that you plug in. A router and an adapter will run you about $200 or less.

The must-have software

OK, we've talked all about the hardware; now, it's time for software. There is really very little software that you need to run your Mary Kay business. However, it is important that you have as close to the most current versions of your software as possible. For instance, if you have Microsoft® Publisher 2000 you might want to consider upgrading to Microsoft® Publisher 2003. The enhancements to the program are significant, but besides that, the more current your program, the more guaranteed you are to be able to convert older files in it. For instance, have you ever received an e-mail from one of your sister Directors that had an attachment that was created in Publisher (or Word) and when you tried to open it, you weren't able to view it? That is because you have an incompatible version of the program that it was created in. If you have the most current version of the software, you will have no problem opening files created on someone else's computer.

These are my suggestions for the necessary software on your computer to run your business effectively:

- **Microsoft® Word 2003**: This is your word processing program to type up letters, flyers and anything else you can think of. You can also use Corel WordPerfect® 12 if you are more used to that program because of your experience in the corporate world. Either way, you need to have a good word processor.

- **Microsoft® Publisher 2003**: This is a must for several reasons. First of all, I think it is the best publishing program on the market. You can create flyers, newsletters, business cards, stationary, postcards, calendars, even websites – all with lots of graphics and designs and it makes you look like a professional graphics designer. I have created several newsletters for Directors in the past and they are all amazed at how incredibly talented I am. But, truth be told, it's about 25% me and 75% Microsoft® Publisher! Also, if you decide you want to use One-Click Newsletters, you must have Publisher installed to make it work.
- **Adobe Acrobat Reader® 6.X**: This is a FREE program that you download from the Web that allows to read PDF files. Let me explain. PDF stands for "Portable Document Format." Say that you create a great flyer for an upcoming event in Publisher and you want to e-mail it to everyone you know. However, some of your sister Directors do not have Microsoft® Publisher on their computers, so when they try to open your great flyer, their computer doesn't recognize it. What you can do is convert that file into a PDF document using a PDF converter (read the next bullet about where to find a PDF converter) and then send it to everyone. Adobe Acrobat Reader® is the program that allows anyone to open and view these PDF files. You probably have already come across this program. If you don't have the latest version, go to www.adobe.com and download it.
- **PDF995® Converter and Printer Driver**: This is another FREE program that converts any document into a PDF file. Basically, when you create a document in Word or Publisher, instead of saving it as a Word or Publisher file, you go to the print command and choose *pdf995*. It then automatically converts your document into a PDF file and opens it in Adobe Reader®. Go to the PDF995® website (http://site4.pdf995.com/download.html) and download the printer driver and the converter. Follow the instructions as to how to install it and use it. It is free but every time you use it, a web page will pop

up advertising the product. If you want to stop that page from popping up, you can purchase the registration key for the program for $9.95.

- **Boulevard®**: This is a must! This program is essential for keeping track of every aspect of your Mary Kay business. The program is incredibly powerful and easy to use and is being updated all the time. This is how the Boulevard® people describe their product:
    - *"Boulevard® automates and streamlines all aspects of your customer tracking, invoicing, product ordering, and inventory management. It also includes unique calendar and address list features which help you manage your time and keep track of important dates and people. You can also track your business expenses and manage your team and unit directly in Boulevard®."*[6]
    - You can copy and paste your customers and product orders from www.marykayintouch.com, you can import your reports from Desktop Office Manager® so all of your unit information is together, you can enter Weekly Accomplishment Sheet results for your unit members and print out monthly recognition reports, along with a slew of other things.
    - There are other programs out there like this but nothing can match the power and ease of Boulevard®. You need to purchase it and learn how to use it. They offer DVD training for a nominal fee and have also started regional training seminars around the country.
- **Anti-Virus Software**: This is also a MUST! In today's world, unfortunately there are evil people out there who have nothing better to do than figure out a way to destroy your computer by circulating viruses on the internet. I can't tell you how many Mary Kay Directors had serious problems with their computers last year because of the KlezWorm. Perhaps even you were a victim of it. I get a virus in an e-mail EVERY DAY. Sometimes I get three or

four EVERY DAY! Luckily, my anti-virus software detects it and then deletes it (or quarantines it) immediately so it never infiltrates my system. There are two main anti-virus programs out there: Symantec's Norton Anti-Virus® and McAfee Virus Scan®. Either one of these programs will be fine. They will prompt you to download the fixes against new viruses on a regular basis so you are always protected. Make sure your anti-virus software is always up and running.

- **SpyBot Search and Destroy®**: This is a FREE program which you download that wipes out SpyWare. What is SpyWare, you ask? I will quote a review written by ZDNET – a technology website:
    - *"If spam is your personal nightmare, consider the havoc adware or spyware may wreak. These tiny applications either feed advertising to software already running on your computer or, worse, collect data about your Internet surfing habits, then broadcast that data to marketers worldwide. Often, you don't even realize that you've installed these apps because they either piggyback on free software that serves another purpose (say, the ad-serving app Cydoor, which is included with the Kazaa file-sharing program) or, often, download and install via nefarious Web sites (notice a new default home page or search engine for your Internet Explorer?). The end result is that your browser may default to unusual search-engine sites or produce odd search results, and you may see exponential growth in the number of pop-up ads that litter your desktop while you surf."*[7]
    - SpyWare also slows your computer down. It can also cause little annoying things to happen like programs freezing up or your computer shutting down unexpectedly.
    - Anyone that uses the internet needs this program. You can find SpyBot Search and Destroy® at http://download.com.com/3000-8022-10122137.html.

Run the program once every week or two for maximum effectiveness.

- **Pop-up Blocker**: Are you not incredibly annoyed when you are innocently surfing the internet and all of a sudden an advertisement appears on your screen in front of what you were looking at? Those are Pop-up ads and you can download one of several FREE blockers that can eliminate these ads entirely. The highest rated Pop-up Blocker is called STOPzilla®. In fact, their latest download includes adware and spyware destroying capabilities as well. Go to www.stopzilla.com to download their program.

Cleaning house – removing unnecessary files

So we've talked all about hardware and software and now I want to discuss how you can organize your computer. The thing about computers is that you don't really see the clutter. Everything is all hidden away, sometimes you don't even know where. However, it is important that you "clean house" every once in a while to keep your computer running smoothly and efficiently so that you can easily find whatever it is you are looking for.

First I want to talk about clutter in your computer. The most obvious area is on your desktop. If you don't know, the desktop is the screen you see after you've booted up your computer that has little icons (or shortcuts) to the programs and files you use most often. This desktop can accumulate a lot of icon clutter. Many times when you install a software program into your computer, it automatically puts an icon on your desktop for that program. It can also put a slew of other icons of programs that they are affiliated with. For instance, a program may offer a special on an AOL membership which has nothing to do with the program you installed, but it will put an AOL icon on your desktop "enticing" you to try their offer. The more programs you install on your computer, the more icons you have on the desktop and after a while your desktop is filled with pictures! This is visual clutter and just like physical clutter, it can make you anxious and uncomfortable.

So it's time to clean up your desktop. The only icons that should be on there are the ones for shortcuts to the programs that you use the most. You might want to keep the Desktop Office Manager®, Boulevard®, Publisher, Word, and your internet service provider icons but many of the rest can go. If you remove the icon, you are NOT removing the program – only the shortcut to get to the program. If you click on the *Start Menu* at the bottom left of the page and then choose *Programs*, you will see folders that hold all of your programs that you can access easily.

To remove icons from your desktop, put your cursor over it, *right*-click on it and select *delete*. A box will come up confirming your deletion. Hit *OK* and move on to the next one. The icons will then be stored in your recycle bin. When you are finished with your clean up, *right*-click on the recycle bin and choose *empty the recycle bin*. That way, you are permanently getting rid of those pesky little icons and it won't take up any more space on your hard drive and desktop.

One icon/shortcut that can be helpful on your desktop is a folder where you store your most used documents – like orientation packets, newsletters, postcard templates, etc. In order to create a folder on your desktop, *right*-click anywhere on the desktop that is free and clear. A menu will pop up – choose *New* and then *Folder*. You will see a new folder on your desktop named "New Folder". *Left*-click on that once and type in your own name like "MK Documents" or "Postcards" or anything you want. Then when you save a document that you will use frequently, you can save it there. I will tell you how later.

Some "hidden" pockets of clutter are "temporary files" and "cookies." These little unseen files clog up your hard drive and can make your computer run slowly. Temporary files are "in preparation" or "just in case" files that get stored on your hard drive when you install a program in the computer. When a program is installing, it needs to create a space for which to do all of its work. It puts some startup files and system files in that space so that as it is installing, it can access them easily. The thing is that once the program is installed, those temporary files are no longer needed. A temporary file is any file that has the *.tmp extension on it. Every file with that extension can be deleted safely from your hard drive.

Cookies are little memories of your times spent surfing the internet. Whenever you go to a site that has lots of pictures and it takes a while to load, or you enter your information in a form on a web page, those pictures and text get saved on your hard drive as a cookie so that the next time you visit that page, it will come up faster, or when you fill out a form, you will only need to type in the first letter of your name and your name will appear in full in the box. These cookies are cute but can again be safely deleted without any trouble.

So what you want to do about once a month is clean out your hard drive of these unnecessary files. Windows® XP, ME and, I even think 2000, all have a utility called *Disk Cleanup* and what it does is search out all these unnecessary files and deletes them for you. In order to do this, click the *Start* menu at the bottom left of the screen and choose *Programs*. From there find the *Accessories* folder and choose *System Tools*. In the *System Tools* folder you will find *Disk Cleanup*. When you click on that, it will take a few minutes for the utility to search your hard drive but when it's done, a menu will pop up to show you what files are available for deletion. These are the files you can safely delete:

- Temporary Internet Files
- Recycle Bin
- Temporary Files
- WebClient/Publisher temporary files
- Compress old files

You will have the choice to delete Setup files as well – these are the bigger files that programs use to install or uninstall themselves, however I tend to leave them on there just in case I want to uninstall a program without using the original CD. Make sure you have a check next to each of the above items and then click *OK*. The utility will delete those files for you and voilá! Your hard drive is free of unnnecessary clutter!

You should also delete any programs that you don't use anymore. They take up valuable hard drive space. For instance, when you install the latest version of AOL®, it does not install itself OVER the old version. It just puts the new version in. Therefore, even though you only use the new version, the old version is still sitting there on your hard drive taking up space. Windows has come up with a very helpful utility called *Add/Remove Programs* where you can completely delete programs that you are not using anymore. Click on the *Start* menu and open up the *Control Panel.* In the *Control Panel* you will see *Add/Remove Programs.* When you click on that a list will pop up of all the programs on your hard drive. Scan down the list and find the programs you no longer need. Click on that program and hit *Change/Remove.* It will ask you to confirm the deletion of the program for which you will click *OK* and it will begin deleting it. As the deletion process goes on, sometimes you will be asked about a shared file and whether or not you really want to delete that particular file because it may be used by another program. It will tell you what to do if you are not sure and then you should just follow those instructions.

You should also optimize your hard drive by defragmenting it about once a month. You can think of this like so: when you take files out of your file cabinet and put it on your desk, or on the floor, or in your briefcase, or in another room – you've created clutter and left holes in your filing cabinet. What defragmentation does is put all of your files away and reorganizes them. We call this "optimizing" your hard drive because when it is organized, it runs better. Windows has again provided you with a utility that does this for you. Click the *Start* menu at the bottom left of the screen and choose *Programs.* From there find the *Accessories* folder and choose *System Tools.* In the *System Tools* folder you will find *Disk Fragmenter.* Click that and when the utility pops up, click the *Defragment* button and the process will begin. This process usually takes a very long time (sometimes hours) – the bigger your hard drive, the longer it takes. So what I do is start it just before I leave my office for the night and let it work while I'm sleeping. By the time I get up in the morning, my hard drive is optimized!

You have to think of your computer like you think about your car. It needs to routine maintenance to keep running smoothly. When you delete unnecessary temporary files and programs and optimize your hard drive on a regular basis, you are extending the working life of your computer.

Organizing your documents (after first finding them)

Now let's talk about folders. You can organize all the documents in your computer just like you organize all the documents in your file cabinet. The first thing you need to do, however is find them! Most of the time when you save a document from Word or Publisher or other such program, it will automatically save itself into a folder called *My Documents*. This folder may be sitting on your desktop if you have an earlier version of Windows. If you have XP, click on the *Start* menu and you will see the *My Documents* folder right there. If you open that folder you will see some subfolders and probably lots of files (especially if you've had your computer for a while). Look at the subfolders. You will see one called *My Pictures* and another called *My Music*. There may be other folders as well, but those are some of the default folders. You may wonder how those files get in there. This is how:

Say you are writing a letter in Microsoft® Word and you want to save it to finish it later. When you click on *File* and then *Save,* a Save box pops up. At the bottom of the box, it asks you what to call the file and at the top of the box, where you want to store it. On the left side of that box you will see icons for *My Computer*, *My Documents*, and *Desktop*. These are all possible places to save your files. If you click on the *My Documents* icon, in the center of the box you will see all of the folders and any other files that you currently have stored in *My Documents*. If you go no farther and just name your letter (and make it a name you will remember) and then click *Save*, your letter will be saved in the *My Documents* folder. (Try this – make up a test page in Word and follow the above instructions. Then open up your *My Documents* folder from the *Start* menu and you should see it there.) Or you can choose to save that document in the "MK Documents" folder you created on your desktop. Just click on the *Desktop* icon at the left of the Save box and now in the body of the box you should see your "MK Documents" folder. Double-click on that folder to select it and then name your document and click *Save.*

When you scan in pictures or download pictures from the internet, they automatically save in the *My Pictures* folder which is a sub-folder of *My Documents.* Just remember that if you want to find a picture, you must first look in *My Documents* and then *My Pictures.*

However, you should organize your *My Documents* folder just like you organize your filing cabinets. Make sub-folders that separate your documents into like groups – "Selling Ideas," "E-mails," "New Consultant Training." You create new folders in *My Documents* the same way you created a new folder on your Desktop. Open up the *My Documents* folder from the *Start* menu then *right*-click anywhere in that box that is free. A menu will pop up – choose *New* and then *Folder.* You will see a new folder on your desktop named "New Folder". *Left*-click on that once and type in your own name as suggested above. Now when you save anything select that folder from the list by double-clicking on it and soon all of your files will be organized.

If you have a lot of files that need to be organized right now, this is how you can do that. Find the *My Computer* icon. It will either be on your desktop or in the *Start* menu. *Right*-click on it and choose *Explore.* Now you will see a pop-up that shows a list of icons on the left side of the screen that represent your desktop and your drives (hard drive, CD Rom drive, floppy disk drive). On the right side of the screen you will see larger icons representing the same things. When you click on anything on the left part of the screen, all of its components will show up on the right side of the screen. Click on the *Documents* folder on the left of the screen. It might be called *My Documents* or it might be called *"Your Name's" Documents*. When you click on that you will see all the contents of that folder – sub-folders and files. Here again, you can create a new folder the same way you have on your desktop to separate files. Now find a file in the *Documents* folder that you would like to put in the new folder you just created. Click and hold on that file then drag it to the new folder. You will notice the new folder will become highlighted when you are holding the file over it. Un-click it and your file will drop into the folder. If you now double-click on that folder, you should see your file. Continue to do this until your entire *Documents* folder is organized.

If you want to move some files from the *Documents* folder to the "MK Documents" folder you created on your desktop, in the *Explore* menu, find the document you want to move (click on *Documents* on the left side of the screen and search for your document on the right side of the screen). Between the left side and right side of the screen you will see a scroll bar that will allow you to view the top or bottom of the left menu. Scroll until you can easily see the "MK Documents" folder (which should appear at the bottom of the list). Then from the right side of the screen, click and drag your file over to the left side of the screen onto the "MK Documents" folder. When you unclick it, it will drop into that folder.

Taking time to organize your files and folders in your computer will pay off big time in the long run. You will always be able to keep track of what you have on your computer without feeling like they disappear, never to be seen again!

Dealing with e-mail clutter

The last great clutter collector in your computer is your e-mail folders. First of all, you must get in the habit of treating your Inbox like you treat every piece of paper that comes across your desk. You have three choices as to what to do – File it, Act on it, or Delete it. If you want to save an e-mail because it is a great selling or recruiting idea from a sister Director, then open it up, click *File*, then *Save As* and save it in an appropriate folder. If the e-mail requires you to respond, do so immediately! If you don't, putting it off will surely result in it being forgotten about completely. If you know that you do not need this e-mail, delete it immediately.

The tricky thing about e-mail is that when you delete a message, it is not actually deleted! When you delete a message, it gets moved to the "trash" or "deleted items folder". It stays there until you empty the trash or until you re-boot your machine! Another little ditty is the fact that every time you send an e-mail, a copy of that message gets saved in the "sent folder". You should make a habit of deleting all the messages permanently from both of these folders. Your e-mail program should give you directions as to how to so this. Try to do it once a week.

One incredibly annoying thing about e-mail these days is the overloading of spam – these unsolicited ads that are the electronic version of telemarketing. If you are overrun with spam, consider changing your e-mail address. Sign up for an alternative name in your current Internet Service Provider plan or change ISP's all together. If you think it is too much hassle to change your e-mail address (although this is the most effective way to combat the problem) you can download a program called SAproxy-Pro®. It is good for spam catching and you can customize it to make certain addresses go permanently to spam or certain addresses NEVER go to spam. It can be downloaded free from the web, (http://downloads-zdnet.com.com/SAproxy-Pro/3000-2382-10298204.html) but after 30 days you have to pay for it – about $30.00. Or if you can afford a little more money, purchase a program called Norton Internet Security put out by Symantec®. Within this program is a Spam Blocker and Norton Anti-Virus. It is very effective and kills two birds with one stone (the virus bird and the spam bird). You can purchase this program at your favorite computer store or online (www.symantec.com).

Well, in this incredibly long-winded chapter, we've covered the main points about computers and the maintenance of them. There is one last thing I want you to do. If you are not computer savvy, please, please LEARN! Ask your children, ask a fellow Director or a consultant in your unit, or take a class. Mary Kay has been very proactive in this by creating lessons in LearnMK®. Do whatever you can to feel comfortable on the computer because it is the lifeline of your office. If you have problems with certain software programs, call Technical Support. That is how I learned how to use the computer. Every time, I couldn't do something, I would call Technical Support and they talked me through it. That way I got to know the computer better and eventually I could solve the problems myself. However you learn, DO IT! I promise it is training you will never regret.

Your Image on Paper

Image is a huge issue in Mary Kay, as you know. You teach your Consultants about the importance of creating a positive image; from the specific uniform requirements to the significance of always maintaining an optimistic attitude. However, just as important as wearing your Director's suit at all company events and Unit Meetings, is how you present yourself on paper. That is the main focus of this chapter.

Why do you require your consultants to wear a skirt or a suit to Unit Meetings and Events? I have always been told that it is because you want guests to take you seriously as business women. NSD Jan Thetford said that what you wear and how you present yourself is so important because you may be the only Mary Kay woman that person will ever meet. First impressions are so important so why would you not use that same thought on the image you project with every document you create and send out? For example, when you prepare your newsletter, do you cut out pictures from other newsletters, and tape them into your master copy? Do you simply copy a page from someone else's newsletter and stick it in yours? When you prepare your orientation packets, do you copy the same pages from copies which are copied from other copies so that now when you copy it, there are little areas of darkness on the page or the text is tilted? When you send out e-mails to people do you **ALWAYS USE BOLD, UNDERLINED, CAPITALIZED PRINT? OR DO YOU SAVE THIS FOR YOUR NEWSLETTER?**

What you create for people to look at, from the outfit you wear, to your manicured nails, to the documents you give them, it all leaves a lasting impression on them. You want to be taken seriously as a legitimate business woman and that concept is all inclusive – from the close-toed shoes to the stationery.

Newsletters

I have seen more "copied and pasted" newsletters than I care to admit. I certainly understand that "in the old days" that was the only thing you could do. However, these days with the power and efficiency of computers and programs like Microsoft® Publisher, there just isn't any excuse for this. It is so simple to create beautiful, professional, and creative newsletters in Publisher that make you look like you sent them to a qualified publisher/printer. You can scan in pictures and manipulate them; you can save any picture that you see on the internet and use it in your publications; you can digitally copy and paste other Director's documents that are found online and change the font so that it matches yours to include in your newsletter. Here are the guidelines you should consider when you create your newsletter:

1. Always use the same fonts throughout the newsletter. Choose one font for all the headings in the newsletter and one font for the body of each of the "articles" in the newsletter. For instance:
    a. *This may be a good heading font (Monotype Corsiva)*
        i. And this may be a good body font (Garamond)
    b. **This may be a good heading font (Impact)**
        i. And this may be a good body font (Times New Roman)

    Whatever you do, make sure you stick to your font scheme throughout your entire newsletter – this includes things like your calendar. This provides professionalism and continuity. Microsoft® Publisher offers several font schemes for publications and you can change them easily by going to the *Format* menu, choosing *Publication Designs* and then *Font Schemes*.
2. In the important task of making sure your fonts are consistent throughout, it is imperative that you do not simply copy a page out of someone else's newsletter and staple it into yours. This looks messy, thrown-together and unprofessional. Re-type whatever it is you want to

include, in your fonts, with your headings, right into your newsletter. If you find something online that was created by another Director, you can often select the text (click and drag from the beginning of the text to the end of the text until it is highlighted) and then copy it (*right*-click on the highlighted text and select *copy*). You can then paste it directly into your newsletter (open your newsletter and *right*-click the spot you want to paste into – select *paste* and it should appear). Change the fonts and spacing so it fits into your publication.

3. Unless you use the One-Click® Newsletter that Mary Kay provides, retype all of your reports results rather than taping them into your master copy making sure that again the fonts match. It may seem like this is unnecessary and a waste of time; However, it makes all the difference in the professional image of the newsletter. This is a much easier task than you may think with Microsoft® Publisher. The table making tool is extremely easy to use and fill in. Check out the help menu if you don't know how to do it. Also, make sure you create your own calendar and enter the company events and your unit events in it, again using the same fonts as the body of your newsletter. Publisher has a calendar making tool that is also very easy to use.
4. **<u>DO NOT USE TOO MANY FORMATTING TOOLS TOGETHER IN THE BODY OF YOUR TEXT. THIS IS VISUALLY MESSY AND OFTEN DIFFICULT TO READ IF THERE IS AN ENTIRE PARAGRAPH WRITTEN THIS WAY. IT ALSO GIVES THE IMPRESSION OF YELLING AT YOUR READER.</u>** Choose to use only one formatting element at a time (**Bold**, <u>underline</u>, *italics*, or CAPITALIZATION) for emphasizing a word or a phrase.
5. For continuity throughout your newsletter, have a title bar on each page of your newsletter that either is the title of the first item on the page ("Contests" or "On-Target Star Consultants", etc.) or is the name of your unit in small letters in the upper right or left of each page. If you

use Microsoft® Publisher and use one of their Newsletter templates, the name of your unit will automatically be entered on each page. Again, make sure that the title bars are all in a consistent font and size.

So you've read this section and you surely think I am crazy. You hardly have any time to simply put together a newsletter not to mention having to retype every little thing that goes in it. Well, if that is what you are thinking, you MUST delegate this task. If your assistant is adept at Publisher (and hopefully she is!) make sure you demand these guidelines from her. Or hire someone else to do it. If you can't find someone to do it rather inexpensively for you, then check out Unit News (www.UnitNews.com). This is a service that creates online newsletters for an extremely reasonable fee (even cheaper than I charge). You send in your recognition reports, promotions, training and opening letter (even pictures!) and they put all the rest of the information together along with all the current company promotions in a clean, easy to read format. They then send you the finished newsletter via e-mail and you can simply forward it to your consultants with e-mail addresses or print it out and copy it for the consultants who aren't online. The only disadvantage of this service is that you don't really have any creative freedom as to the character and look of the newsletter. The template they use is the same for everyone. However, it is a way to delegate this monthly task and look professional.

Orientation and Training Packets

The same guidelines as laid out above apply to your Orientation and Training Packets. How long has it been since you've updated your packets? Remember this is often the very first thing your New Consultant sees from you. That first impression is extremely important! Have you been copying pages from copies that have been copied from copies? Is any of the information in your packets outdated and you have had to manually cross out and change them? If any of these things are true, you need to have your packets redone. Again, delegate this task to your assistant or someone else who is experienced with the computer. Create your packets with as much care as you create your newsletter. Retype pages that were borrowed from someone else so that your character shows through. Make sure all the fonts match throughout and that you have the most current and updated information.

Stationery

Do you have your own Signature Stationery? If not, you should. Every time you hand a packet to someone or send a postcard or letter, you should put it on your personal stationery. That way, your mail stands out above the rest and is easily recognizable. The front page of your packets should be printed on your stationery. When you send out love notes to your unit, they should be on your stationery. When you send On Target Star Consultant postcards or I1, 2, 3, and T letters, they should be on your stationery.

You do not have to spend a lot of money on stationery. The Mary Kay stationery is beautiful and certainly many Directors use it. You can also find a huge selection of stationary at Paper Direct (www.paperdirect.com) with all sorts of extras. You can even go to your favorite office supply store and find stationery there. However, if you don't want to invest a great deal of money, you can create your own fabulous stationery! If you have Microsoft® Publisher (which you should!) you can either create your own letterhead and postcards or you can use one of their many stationary set templates. That way, your template is always in your computer and then when you need to send a letter or postcard you can type right into your template or print out a letterhead and write it by hand.

Your image in e-mail and on the web

This chapter is called *Your Image on Paper* but I feel we need to address your image on *electronic* paper as well. What am I talking about? Does this look familiar? FW:FW:FW:FW:FW:

When you receive an e-mail that has this type of subject line you may immediately throw it out. You may take the time to read it but you had to scroll through the hundreds of names and addresses that this e-mail has already reached. And on top of that, the original message has been sent so many times, you may see << at the beginning of every truncated line of the text. This is ridiculous and unnecessary. No matter how "good" the e-mail is, by forwarding it this way, you are disrespecting the information not to mention disrespecting the person (or persons) you are sending it to. That is why 60% to 70% of these types of e-mails go unread.

First you need to make sure that you do not just forward everything you get in your inbox to everyone you know. Just as when you are determining whether a piece of paper in your office is important enough to keep, make that kind of distinction in your e-mail. Ask yourself, "Is this important enough to send to my unit? My sister Directors? Can they find this information elsewhere? Will this inspire them to be or do better?" If you deem this e-mail important enough to forward, then prepare it for sending by cleaning up all of the "postmarks." First of all, when you hit the *Forward* button, immediately change the subject line of the message so it doesn't say FW:. Change the subject so it sounds like it is a personal e-mail from you. Then, in the body of the message, delete all of the addresses of the previous recipients and add a personal message at the top of the body of the e-mail that tells your readers why you thought this was important enough to send on to them. Then, if necessary, adjust the formatting of the e-mail by removing any << markings and unnecessary spacing that makes the message difficult to read. I promise that the e-mails that you send will have much more of an impact if you take these small steps.

Lastly, I want to mention UnitNet (www.unitnet.com). This online venue is an excellent tool for Mary Kay Directors and Consultants. However, if you decide to open up a UnitNet site, you have to look at it as your virtual online office and it needs to be organized as such. First of all, make sure you update it regularly. There's nothing more disappointing than going onto a site in May when the latest information provided is from March. If you are going to commit to this form of communication, make sure you update it at least once a month when your monthly reports come out, but I would suggest updating it with a personal message at least every two weeks, if not every week.

Second of all, organize the sections of your site like you would your filing cabinet. For instance, in the "Training" area, organize all of your documents into categories – "Selling Ideas," "Inspiration," "Recruiting Ideas," etc. Then when anyone needs to find a certain document they will easily find it in the appropriate category rather than having to scroll though an incredibly long list. Also, make sure that if you use pictures, they are not blurry and distorted. If you don't know how to properly upload your pictures so that they are clear and proportionate, contact technical support of UnitNet. They will gladly answer any of your questions. For that matter, make sure you learn everything you can about how to set up and organize your site so that you can present your best image. If you don't feel like you have the skills to do this on your own, hire someone to do it for you.

Take the time to work on your image on paper (electronic or otherwise). Remember that every time you put your name on something, it speaks volumes about you. Image is about presenting yourself in a way that people will take you seriously. You realize its importance in other aspects of your Mary Kay business – make it just as important in this.

The Assistant – You Need One!

So you want to be a National Sales Director. Or, perhaps your goals are not quite as lofty. Maybe you just want to be a Million Dollar Director. Maybe you want to be in the $350,000 Unit Club. Maybe you want to qualify for the Grand Prix. Maybe you are a new Director and you want to be in the Fabulous 50's Club. Whatever your goal is, how are you going to achieve it? What do you have to do in order to reach these goals, big or small? You know the answer to this. You have to get out into the field and meet the people! There's no question about it. You are not going move up in Mary Kay by working in your office.

This means that you must have an assistant. Yes, I said MUST. 85% of all the activities that go on in the office are things that your assistant should be doing so that you can be out meeting women and building your unit and production. Here is a list of all the activities that can be done by your assistant (this list assumes you have Boulevard® up and running):

1. Go through the In/Out File system and complete all Daily tasks including:
    - Entering Customer Profile information in Boulevard®
    - Updating the Customer Lists in InTouch® www.marykayintouch.com for easy PCP enrollment
    - Creating invoices for product sales in Boulevard® to control inventory counts and keep a record of your customer's purchases
    - Processing returned product & Accounts Receivable in Boulevard®
    - Processing New Consultant Agreements – making sure the new Consultant is in Boulevard® and on all of your contact lists and has been tracked as to when they place an order, have their debut, go through training, etc.
    - Entering inventory orders into the computer – desktop office manager and Boulevard®

- Entering Loaned/Borrowed/Exchanged/ Personal Use product into Boulevard® for the purpose of inventory control
- Sending out any product orders to customers
- Printing out Recruit Profiles/Contact lists, production, New Consultant reports, etc and putting them in your Focus Folder
- Downloading Daily Production reports and importing them into Boulevard®
- Processing Weekly Accomplishment Sheets in Boulevard® and Ribbon them (if necessary)

2. Complete Monthly tasks including:
   - Sending out invoices to customers with unpaid balances
   - Preparing Birthday/Anniversary Cards for you to send out to your consultants for the following month – this task is done when the newsletter is being prepared and the dates are being added for the next month
   - Newsletter preparation and creation
   - Printing, labeling, stapling newsletter
   - Printing out Monthly IBM® Reports—Parent Unit Section between the 7th and the 12th of each month
   - Sending out Inactive/Termination Letters or postcards
3. Make sure office space is clean by:
   - Emptying the *To File* folder in the In/Out File System
   - Processing inventory orders, labeling product and putting product away
   - Labeling catalogs
   - Putting away Skin Care Class supplies and Success Meeting supplies
   - Cleaning Face Cases
4. Complete Quarterly tasks including:
   - Sending out On Target Star Consultant postcards

5. Complete tasks as needed including:
   - Copying and assembling Orientation and Training Packets
   - Assembling Hostess/Recruiting Packets
   - Creating posters and literature for Success meetings
   - Calling consultants to update their personal information such as e-mail addresses
   - Ordering business tapes and supplies for the office (including stationery)

Of course, this list is not all inclusive. There are several other tasks that can be done by your assistant but these represent the majority. So, as you read that list, how many of those things have you been doing yourself? Five tasks? Ten tasks? All of the tasks? Do you remember those 3 little letters – **I P A**? None of those tasks listed are **I**ncome **P**roducing **A**ctivities! These tasks are extremely important in order to run an efficient office and successful business, but they are NOT Income Producing.

Hear my heart on this – this is some tough love – if you want to reach your goals in Mary Kay, no matter how big or small, you cannot focus your attention in your office. You MUST meet the women, sell the product, build your unit. You, of course, know this, but if you think back to the last week or so and compare the hours you spent in your office doing those tasks to the hours you spent at selling appointments, getting five or ten new names a day, doing recruiting interviews, which number would be higher? Unfortunately, it is very easy to use office work as an excuse not to grow your business. I mean, how can you even think about going out to get new names when you can't see the top of your desk, you have to send out that order to your best customer, or your newsletter needs to be created and then copied?

You must learn to delegate and feel comfortable with it. Don't be afraid to give up control. I guarantee that when you do learn to delegate, your business will soar because you will finally be free to work toward your goals rather than working against them.

The perfect assistants – Where are they?

OK, hopefully I've convinced you that you need an assistant. Now you're asking, "Where do I get one?" Well, unfortunately this is not always an easy question to answer. It is often a difficult task to find someone, not to mention finding someone who is really good. I will tell you that the best assistants are Consultants. There are obvious reasons for this – they know the product, they know how the business works (selling vs. recruiting), and they know the language. So, the first place you should look is within your unit. Is there a unit member or adoptee that shows up to every meeting with a new flyer that they created that they wanted to share, or they came up with an efficient system for organizing their customer profiles that they can't wait to tell you? This Consultant is organized, motivated and independent and might make a great assistant. Also, if this Consultant wants to move up the Career Path, she will relish the opportunity to be surrounded by someone who is actively achieving their goals – YOU! Remember, that is how I became an assistant – I wanted to succeed in my business, so I knew that I needed to surround myself with success. You might also try talking to one of your customers who seem to be really sharp and who might be able to use some extra money (or product!). Your customers also know the product line and just may have some idea as to how the business works. Who knows, maybe you could recruit her!

If you can't think of a consultant or customer who would work, you can certainly look outside of Mary Kay. You can advertise at a local university – there are always students looking to earn some extra cash. You could advertise in the local newspaper. If you are really desperate, as a last resort, you could call a temp agency in your area. This will cost you, but if you need someone immediately to help you with a project (like reorganizing your office from top to bottom), this is an option.

So, what do you need in an assistant? Well, here is a short list of criteria:

- They must be proficient on the computer. They need to know how to use Microsoft® Word and Microsoft® Publisher because most of your document creation will happen in these two programs. They should also be able to get around the internet very well. It is not necessary that they know Boulevard® or Desktop Office Manager®. They will learn those programs when they start working for you. However, they must be willing and able to learn new programs. Even if your new assistant is not a Consultant, if they are excellent on the computer, the training process will be especially easy.
- They must be willing to commit to a work schedule. You need to make it clear how often you would like them to come in and for how long. You can ask them what their availability is and determine a mutually convenient schedule, but you need to make your expectations clear and get a commitment from them accordingly. If you make it too flexible, they will not consider this a "real" job and not take it seriously. Within a few weeks, you will be more frustrated than productive and your assistant will either leave or you will ask them to.
- They need to be friendly and willing to learn. They need to be independent and eventually be able to anticipate your needs. They need to be willing to take direction.

Interviewing a potential assistant

If finding this "perfect" person seems impossible, have no fear! Be patient. They are out there. You just need to look and be willing to do some interviews. Here are some questions to ask in an interview:

1. Do you have another job?
2. Do you have a family? Young children?

These questions address their potential commitment to you. If they have another job, chances are the hours that they are available would be less convenient for you. They may only have nights or weekends to offer you which may not be as convenient as someone who would be able to come in the daytime during the week. Also, families involving young children or even teenagers have a whole different set of time conflicts (as I'm sure many of you know) which may make it difficult to get a firm time commitment from them.

3. What kind of work experience have you had?
4. Have you ever worked in an office before? In what capacity?

These questions will give you an idea as to whether or not they have any experience to bring to the job. Having to train someone who has never stepped into an office environment or has never had a job can be quite a task. They can be the sweetest and most helpful person but having to teach them to be an office manager may be a task you don't need right now.

5. How proficient are you with the computer?
   a. Do you have a computer at home?
   b. What operating system are you most comfortable with? Windows® XP, 2000, Mac?
   c. Have you ever worked with Microsoft® Word? Microsoft® Publisher?
   d. Have you ever heard of Boulevard®?
   e. Do you have internet access? What is your internet service provider? AOL®? Earthlink®? Optimum Online®?

The computer expertise questions are very important. As I said before, you must hire an assistant who knows what they are doing on the computer. This is especially important if you are not a whiz on the computer yourself. So much of the "business" in your office is on the computer. You must be able to rely on your assistant to take care of it for you. You want to ask them if they have a computer at home for a few reasons. First of all, that will give you an idea if they are used to using one on a regular basis. Second of all, some computer work (like the creation of the monthly newsletter) could conveniently be completed at the home of the assistant. Thirdly, you want to know what kind of programs they are used to using. Many Windows programs are based on the same prototype. If you can get around in Word, chances are you will work just fine in Publisher even if you haven't seen that program before. You also want to know what e-mail service they use because they will be updating your address book with your new consultants and you want to know if they are familiar with how to do that.

6. How much do you know about Mary Kay?
    a. Are you familiar with the product line?
    b. Have you ever been facialed?
    c. Do you know how we sell our product?
    d. Do you know how the position of Director is different than that of a Consultant?

You want to ask them about their knowledge of Mary Kay for obvious reasons. If they don't know about the products, you should facial them! This introduces them to the product line, but more importantly it shows them how you sell the product. They are going to be working for you in your role as the Consultant as well as you in your role as the Director. They need to know how those jobs differ. Obviously, if they don't know anything about the business, this is an area that you can teach very well. But, what you can tell here is whether or not they are interested enough to learn about Mary Kay.

7. If you were to be offered the position, when are you willing and able to work?
    a. Would you be able to come in a few times a week for a few hours each time instead of one long day a week?
    b. Would you be available to attend unit meetings and events on an as needed basis?

Pinning down the availability of a potential assistant is essential. If the schedule they offer is not convenient, determine their willingness to compromise.

8. If you were to be offered the position, what would you expect to be paid?

This will tell you if they have preconceived notions about compensation and whether or not you will be able to meet those expectations. If they give you a high per hourly rate, you can ask them if they would be willing to accept less at first with room for growth as things move along.

9. Do you consider yourself an organized person?

The last two questions address their organizational skills as well as their ability to work independently. First of all, your assistant needs to be at least (but preferably more) as organized as you! If organization is not your thing, you want someone in your office that can keep you on track.

10. If I were to give you several tasks to do, would you feel comfortable being here alone to complete them?

This is a very important point. You want your assistant to manage your office WITHOUT YOU. I hear about more Directors who sit with their assistant and watch over everything they do. That is called micromanagement and goes totally against the purpose of an assistant. If you are there micromanaging every task your assistant does than what are you NOT doing? You are NOT growing your business. The purpose of your assistant is to take care of 85% of the office business so you can be OUT of the office meeting new people. If you are there working with your assistant every hour they are there, why are you paying them? Let them do their job and you do yours.

How often should an assistant work?

That depends on a couple of things. Mary Kay Corporate suggests that you have someone come in one hour a week for every ten Consultants in your unit. That's a good suggestion, but it also depends on how many selling appointments you have. If you have 30 unit members, but you do 3 to 4 selling appointments consistently every week with a strong reorder business, 3 hours a week is probably not enough to process all the customers and products going in and out of your office. If, however, you rarely have a selling appointment, have a mild reorder business and are simply maintaining 30 unit members, than 3 hours a week may be just fine.

Then there is the question, how often should an assistant come in? It may seem logical that, if you only need an assistant for 3 to 4 hours a week, they could come in one day a week. However, I suggest that you break it up into a couple of days a week. Consider this scenario:

You have between 55 and 60 unit members and are actively working as a Consultant doing 2 selling appointments a week. Your assistant comes in every Thursday from 9:00 am to 2:00 pm. It's the third week of the month; you had a skin care class on Thursday night (3 guests, $400) and Saturday afternoon (5 guests, $600), you've recruited 2 new unit members, you need to place an inventory order and your newsletter information needs to be gathered so your assistant can create it next week. You know that, next Thursday, your assistant will have to spend most of her time generating your newsletter, but in the meantime, you have a pile of unprocessed work – 8 new customers to be processed and followed up, $1000 in product sales to be processed, 2 new unit members to add to the database and contact lists and to be followed up with, a pending inventory order (which can't be accurate because the product that you just sold hasn't been processed, so you don't know what you currently have on your shelf), and your newsletter hasn't been started yet. So, it's Monday. What do you do? Do you wait for your assistant to come in on Thursday and beg them to stay longer so they can catch up before they begin the newsletter? Most likely, you won't do that. Most likely, you will sit at your computer for hours doing all those processing tasks yourself just so you can stay on top of things. But then, what is the purpose of having an assistant? You just did their job for them. And it wasn't really your fault. It was simply bad scheduling.

A better scenario is to have your assistant come in on Monday from 9:00 am to 11:30 am and Thursday from 9:00 am to 11:30am. That way the daily processing tasks (customer profiles, product sales and orders, new consultants) can be done as the work comes in and it doesn't pile up. This makes your assistant feel more confident in their job and you are not as overwhelmed in your office.

How much should you pay?

Now that you've found someone you really like and they have committed to a schedule that is mutually convenient, you need to decide what you are going to pay them. Well, there are a couple of things to consider. Their experience counts as well as their skills. Their commitment should also be a major factor. If you hire someone whom you suspect may call to cancel or reschedule frequently (which hopefully you won't do), that person should not be offered as much as someone you know will be there when they say. Minimum wage is between $5.50 and $6.50 but remember, you are not asking this person to flip burgers. This job requires some skill, organization, and creativity and deserves to be compensated accordingly. If you hire a college student who has little office experience, but is competent on the computer, willing to learn, and responsible, you could easily offer them between $8 and $10 an hour. If they are exceptional at the computer and demonstrate that they learn quickly, you might want to offer them up to $12 an hour. If you hire someone who has been an office assistant before or has worked in the corporate world with a good job history, is an expert on the computer and possesses an independent spirit, you could offer them $15 an hour without hesitation. After all, this person will quickly take on the role of office manager, controlling that aspect of your business so you don't have to.

You must also be prepared to compensate them for time that they are working for you outside of your office. For instance, if they create your newsletter at their home, or they come to your unit meeting to assist you, you obviously need to pay them for that time. You might also expect that if you send out your assistant on errands, they have the right to charge you for their time, especially if it is a task like taking your newsletter to a copy center to copy, collate, staple and fold; a job that takes time and is certainly something you don't want to be doing. If however, you are uncomfortable with paying for these outside services at the hourly rate, decide not to give these tasks to your assistant. The newsletter ordeal, for example, can easily be done by the copy center and it might be a little cheaper than paying your assistant to do it. Drop it off and pick it up later.

Make sure your assistant fills out weekly time sheets for you that include all the in-office and out-of-office (if any) hours. That way you will be able to see exactly how many hours they are working, providing you with a financial record of it for tax purposes. Don't forget to tell your assistant that she needs to process this invoice as an office expense in Boulevard® so that it is included in your tax reports at the end of the year.

No matter what you originally offer your assistant, it is extremely important that every 6 months you review their work and your production and consider giving them a raise. Yes, that's right. I said, "You should give them a raise if it is warranted". What is supposed to happen is this: you get an assistant so you can get out of your office and meet the people. You do exactly that. You meet new women, recruit new unit members, your production increases and you are on the fast track to achieving your goals. The reason all of this is possible is because your assistant is managing your office smoothly so you don't have to think twice about it. If your production has increased by 10% or more in the last 6 months, don't you think your assistant deserves a reward? The more you offer that assistant, the more they will give you in time, attitude, and performance. This is a MUST!

Communicating with your assistant

There are just a few other things to think about when it comes to appropriately managing your assistant. One of the most important things you need to know is to how to communicate with them. Remember that, no matter how exceptional this person is, they can't read your mind. Every time you write something down for them, be very clear. Here are some things I have come across in other Director's offices that you need to consider:

- Good penmanship is a must. I know that when you are at a skin care class and writing sales tickets as fast as you can, the last thing you are thinking about is whether or not your "n" looks like an "n" or an "x". However, you have to remember that, in a few days, your assistant is going to be looking at that sales ticket to enter the customer information and products into Boulevard® and if they can't read it, they won't be able to complete the task, which wastes time. When you get home that night, look over those tickets and print clearly over anything that is illegible or ambiguous.
- SH makes perfect sense to you. You've been writing SH for years. However, your new assistant may not be a consultant, or not have been in the business long enough to know that SH is an abbreviation for Satin Hands® Pampering Set. Remember that everything you write is going to have to be read and understood by someone else. Be clear. Later on, the two of you will get to know the abbreviations together and you can return to your shorthand.
- Copper Beach, Sunny Spice and Red Salsa all refer to the cosmetic line, obviously. However, your assistant may not know right off the bat that one is an eye color, one is a cheek color, and one is a lip color. When they are creating invoices for your customers, they have to look up each color individually and if they don't know what category to look in, there will be a lot of wasted time. When you hire them, give them an order sheet and have them study all

the color products so they become familiar with them. At first, assume your assistant doesn't know the difference between a Pink Pout Lip Gloss and a Pink Ice Lipstick.

- Remember that you have medium-coverage, full-coverage, and dual-coverage foundations on your shelf. When you write "300" on a sales ticket or profile, your assistant may know that it is a Beige 300 foundation, but she doesn't know if it is medium, full, or dual. Be specific for the sake of your inventory.
- Mark very clearly on the sales ticket if an item has been given away for free or if it has been discounted. These things need to be reflected in Boulevard® for tax purposes.
- Make sure you mark whether a sale has been paid for or not. This is especially important for reorders because you want to have a record of who still owes you money. In Boulevard®, if a customer owes you, their name appears in red in the customer list. If they have paid, your assistant needs to clear their account.

Finally, the last thing I want to address is the issue of respect for both your assistant and their time, which may seem obvious to you, but is very important. In Mary Kay, there are many times when we find ourselves project driven rather than time driven. For example, an event is coming up and the preparations are all consuming and have an immediate deadline. You need your assistant to create the flyers, package the product gifts, call the venue, process the incoming ticket orders, etc. This is all on top of the daily tasks that need to be handled in your office. You, as the Director, are used to just working through until the project is done – because you have to. However, your assistant committed a certain number of hours a week to you because she has a family, another job, a life.... This doesn't mean, of course, that you can't occasionally ask your assistant to stay longer in order to finish the project. However, you need to be considerate of their time and not assume that they will stay for several hours beyond their commitment. Some assistants won't say a word; they want to please you and be as much of a help as possible, so they will stay for an extra three hours. But, you should make it your responsibility to let them know it is OK for them to have boundaries; that they don't have to stay if they can't or don't want to. Always be conscious of their time. If you are, I guarantee they will be eternally grateful and want to do more for you.

So, now you know everything there is to know about assistants (well, almost). Find a good one and enable them to do their job well by being clear in your communication and by letting them do their job without micromanagement. I guarantee, a good assistant can turn your business around 180 degrees (for the better, that is)!

Designing your Day and Life With Value-Driven Time Management

The one thing that I shouldn't really have to teach you is the concept of time management. I mean, you teach time management to your Consultants on a regular basis, right? However, what surprises me so much, when I meet Directors, is that 98% of them don't use a Weekly Plan Sheet! I think the reason for this is that Directors look at time management as a hard and fast schedule that you have to stick to. They believe that life is too ever-changing and it seems impossible to commit to a weekly plan. Let's face it. I've been to those training classes at Company events where they teach about how to use the Weekly Plan Sheet. A wonderfully zealous Director brings in her blown up and laminated chart with blocks of colored markers filling the entire sheet – no white in sight. While, in theory, this system seems utterly logical, in actuality it is overwhelming and difficult to stick to, because these serious schedules often have very little to do with, not only, real life, but more importantly, your values.

What do your values have to do with it? Well, we all have a set of values – principles and standards that guide our lives and our decision-making. What do you think your life would be like if you lived every day to serve your values? Value-driven time management means living every day with a purpose and that purpose is based on your personal value system. I learned about the importance of scheduling your life's activities by focusing on your values in reading Stephen R. Covey's best-seller The 7 Habits of Highly Effective People. Perhaps you have read it. Perhaps it has been on your shelf because someone mentioned it to you, but you haven't yet picked it up. Perhaps you've never heard of it. In any case, I strongly suggest you read it (again, if necessary). If you take all 7 habits to heart, your life and business will change dramatically.

The first step in this process is figuring out what your values are. What is really important to you? What drives you in your relationships, your charity, your business, your life? Write down a list of 5 to 10 values that are important to you. This list could include:

- Friendship
- Family
- Security
- Happiness
- Charity
- Leadership
- Fun
- Freedom
- Spirituality
- Confidence

This list could go on and on. But it is important to write your values down. Seeing them in print solidifies them in your mind and makes them "real."

Now looking at your list, do you live your life by these values? Do you live your life everyday consciously guided by these values? Do you only choose activities according to what is most important to you?

The next step is to write a clarifying statement about each of your values. For instance, if one of your values was friendship, a clarifying statement for that value could be:

> "I am a supportive friend who seeks out friendships that are healthy and encouraging."

Now, take each of your values and write a clarifying statement for each. These statements represent your mission – what drives you. When you have finished these statements then you will draft a personal mission statement. A mission statement is, as Stephen Covey defines it, "your constitution, the solid expression of your vision and values. It becomes the criterion by which you measure everything else in your life."[8] Pretty deep, huh? It is so important to have a mission statement, but so many people don't take the time. A mission statement "can be a powerful tool in providing direction and meaning to life."[9]

What a personal mission statement should focus on is "what you want to be (character) and to do (contributions and achievements) and on the values or principles upon which being and doing are based."[10] So, in order to start thinking about your mission, ask yourself these three questions:

1. Who am I?
2. What values are most important to me?
3. What do I want to contribute to my life and the world based on my values and principles?

One way to clarify your mission statement and make it more balanced is if you divide it up according to the different roles you have in your life. When you define your roles and state your mission for those roles then you can easily focus your goals on your mission. What roles do you have – wife, mother, daughter, Director, Consultant, church member, teacher, leader, friend, household manager, volunteer? Once you identify these roles, you want to think about your long term goals that you want to assign to each of them. These goals will be a part of your mission statement. By defining these roles and goals, you are giving yourself a direction and overall perspective for your life.

There are many ways to write a mission statement. You can write it as a paragraph or group of paragraphs or just in phrases. You can have detailed sections that are centered on each role or you can have a simple paragraph that brings all of your roles together. I encourage you to try it. If you need guidance, log on to the Franklin Covey® website, at http://www.franklincovey.com/missionbuilder/index.html , where you will find a free guided Mission Statement Wizard. When you are finished answering all of the questions, you will have an opportunity to write your own mission statement and they will e-mail a copy of it to you.

There is also a wonderful software program called PlanPlus®. This software program was developed by Stephen Covey's company. It is a wonderful program that supplements Microsoft® Outlook which has many wizards to help you discover your values, write your Mission Statement and schedule your time according to your values and mission.

So, you may be thinking, "All this touchy-feely stuff is great, but how is it going to help me fit in all the things I need to do in my daily schedule?" Well, the point is that, when you are scheduling your life on a daily or weekly basis, you need to make sure you are only engaged in the activities that directly affect your mission.

What you want to do is always "Put First Things First." That is the principle behind Habit 3 in The 7 Habits of Highly Effective People.[11] When you are doing your weekly planning, define the roles from your Mission Statement you will be taking on this week and list what goals that you need to accomplish for each role. Go to your Weekly Plan Sheet and schedule those goals as either an appointment or a task.

Taken from the example above, my value is friendship and my clarifying statement is, "I am a supportive friend who seeks out friendships that are healthy and encouraging." My goal for this week would be, "Call Tamara to ask her how her sick grandmother is doing." I would then schedule that phone call into my Weekly Plan.

By scheduling these activities, you are making small commitments toward your mission, which will lead you directly toward living your life based on your values. This will then result in your biggest goals achieved!

These concepts should not be completely new to you, as the *6 Most Important Things To Do* list is based upon them. As a reminder, this is how it works:

1. At the top of the page, you write out your most immediate goal.
2. In the splatter list below that, you write down everything you feel that you need to do that day.
3. Next to each activity you wrote in the splatter list, you write who you can delegate it to (remember, not everything that needs to be done, needs to be done by you!)
4. Finally, you take the six most important activities that you must do **that directly affect your goal** and write them in the list at the bottom of the page. That is what you should accomplish that day.

Your 6 activities directly affect your goal(s), your goals come directly from your mission and your mission is created around your values. This is the basis of value-driven time management.

So, going back to those multi-colored, blown up, and laminated Weekly Plan Sheets you see from those other Directors, it isn't necessary (and is actually unwise) to schedule every single hour of your day. I don't suggest that you use this method unless you know you can follow it. Instead, use it to schedule your mission-driven activities and your *6 Most Important* activities (which could be one and the same) FIRST. Then, map out your Mary Kay time.

When you map out your Mary Kay time, you know that there are several aspects of your business that you personally need to attend to. As a Director, you need to communicate with your unit via phone or e-mail, plan Unit Meetings, conduct trainings and interviews, and a slew of other activities. As a consultant, you need to schedule selling appointments, perform follow up phone calls, and plan open houses. What I suggest you do is schedule unit time and customer time and stick to that plan. If you say that Monday from 9:00am to 10:30am is unit time, make sure you commit to only doing unit related items in that time. Do not count your inventory, place a product order, package up product for a customer, check your e-mail, etc. Commit to communicating with your unit members or scheduling interviews with your unit members' prospective team members in that time period.

Schedule in correspondence time. Decide when you are going to read and answer your e-mails, listen to your voice mail and return phone calls. If you don't schedule these activities, these activities will schedule you. Also, make sure you commit to one scheduling system – either a datebook or a PDA or the Mary Kay quarterly planner. That way, you will never "forget" something because you forgot to transfer the appointment from one system to another.

This is the most important aspect of Weekly Planning. You are making small commitments to yourself and you need to stick to them. It's not about scheduling every hour of the day. It is about committing a small amount of time to one activity and following through with that commitment. If you plan your time, you achieve your goals step by step. If you don't plan, you spend your entire day putting out fires.

Some other important activities that you need to schedule include:

- 10 or 15 minutes everyday to clean off your desk. Use your In/Out File System (see *The Secret to a Clutter Free Office – The In/Out File System* Chapter for more information) faithfully to complete this task.
- About an hour a week to reorganize your office. Clean out your In/Out File system in this time, making sure the *To Do* and *To File* folders are empty.
- Time to do your Weekly Planning.

Again, when you do these activities, do not allow yourself to become distracted. Follow through and complete them. If you commit to Weekly Planning, I guarantee you will achieve your goals faster!

As I mentioned throughout this chapter, I highly recommend Stephen Covey's The 7 Habits of Highly Effective People. There is so much more than what I covered here that is of great value to anyone. If you want to further discover how these concepts can affect your life, check out the Franklin Covey® website (www.franklincovey.com). You can purchase all the Covey books, planners and accessories; you can even be personally coached by a trained "7 Habits" coach. They also have several advice tools taken directly out of Stephen Covey's books that can guide you to be more effective in your life. Check it out; you won't regret it.

Feng Shui Your Office

I know that some of you are saying, "Feng what?" Feng Shui (pronounced *fuhng shway*) is the ancient Chinese art of placement. Its principles are based on the fact that everything in our environment has energy. In Chinese, that energy is called ch'i (pronounced *chee*). Where you place all of the objects in your environment will affect the flow of the ch'i. When the ch'i flows freely, everybody's happy! When the ch'i gets "stuck", things in your life can get "stuck" as well. Let me assure you that feng shui is not a religion. You do not have to pray to Buddha or any other heavenly body in order for it to work. However, when you apply the principles of feng shui to any space in your home, you will see a significant improvement in your life. I know this because I just feng shui'ed my home with the help of a feng shui consultant.

I always had an interest in the concept of feng shui, but I honestly didn't know much about it until I began writing this book. I had heard about the benefits of it and decided to include a chapter about how to apply it to your office. So, I read several books on the subject and became fascinated with it! I realized that there were several areas in my home that could use a little help in the area of "ch'i flow" and I started to make some changes. I just bought a house a little over a year ago and when I thought back, I realized that very soon after my housemate and I moved into the house, we started having some challenges in our lives. Our careers, our health, our energy, all were affected in a negative way. The more I read about feng shui and how the energy in your home can affect your life so dramatically, I decided that I needed to call in an expert. She came in and went through our home giving us suggestions on specific things that we could adjust in the placement of certain objects in our home. Honestly, when we made those changes, within a few days we felt different. The air in our home seemed "clear"; we had energy to attack and complete projects, we felt more creative and our lives started to change. Within a month, my housemate was offered not only 1 but 2 new jobs and I finished this book and the reviews were exceptional! I know that in the next few months the benefits of this consultation will continue to become evident.

Now, don't worry. I'm not trying to convert you to some weird Chinese ritual. When I read those books and analyzed my own situation, I realized that there could be something to this. Just taking some of my suggestions about your office certainly couldn't hurt anything but more likely will give you a cosmic push in the right direction.

The number one most important aspect of feng shui is the absence of clutter. So, if you have followed all of my instructions in this book so far, you should already be very well on your way to good feng shui! Clutter is nothing but stagnant energy (ch'i) and when the energy is stagnant, your life becomes stagnant. You have already experienced this, I'm sure. If you have lived in a cluttered and disorganized office, you know how being in that office for long periods of time affects you. You feel unmotivated, frustrated, tired; the list goes on. Conversely, if you are in an uncluttered space you instantly feel more at ease, you can think clearly, and you have more energy. Imagine yourself in a clutter-free office; the energy is flowing and you are working efficiently and motivated to achieve your goals! It will happen!

The other two most important aspects of feng shui that pertain to your office involve the entrance of the office and the placement of your desk. Even if you change nothing else in your office (besides removing clutter), address these issues. It could dramatically change your business.

It is very important that every door in your house, and especially your office, is free and clear to open up completely. Doors are very important in feng shui because they allow the ch'i to flow from room to room. If a door cannot open up all the way because it is blocked by a piece of furniture or things hanging on it, the ch'i cannot flow freely and there will be stagnant energy. Take all of those hanging storage bags off the back or front of your doors and remove any obstruction in order to allow the door to open freely. If you cannot walk into your office without having to adjust the direction of your body, you have bad feng shui.

As far as your desk is concerned, the worst placement is facing a wall with your back to the main entrance of the room. The reason for this is that you can easily become startled anytime anyone enters the room; impcnding and real fear create uneasy ch'i. Place your desk out into the room some way so that you are facing the door when you sit at it. If that is an impossibility, place a mirror on your desk facing the door so that when you sit there, you can see who is coming in your office in the mirror. If you are intrigued by feng shui and decide to do some reading on your own, you will find that mirrors are excellent enhancers to many spaces in your home.

Also, make sure your office is well lit with as much natural light as possible. If you have your office in a basement and you don't have any windows, have as many lamps as you can with full spectrum light bulbs in them. It will seem like there is sunlight in your room!

If you start reading about feng shui, you will learn about the bagua (pronounced *bah-gwah*) which is an octagonal chart that shows the nine main areas (or guas) of your life and home. The eight sides of the bagua represent (in clockwise order) prosperity, fame/reputation, relationships/love, creativity/children, helpful people, career, skills and knowledge, and family. The center of the bagua represents health. *See figure 10.1 Bagua*

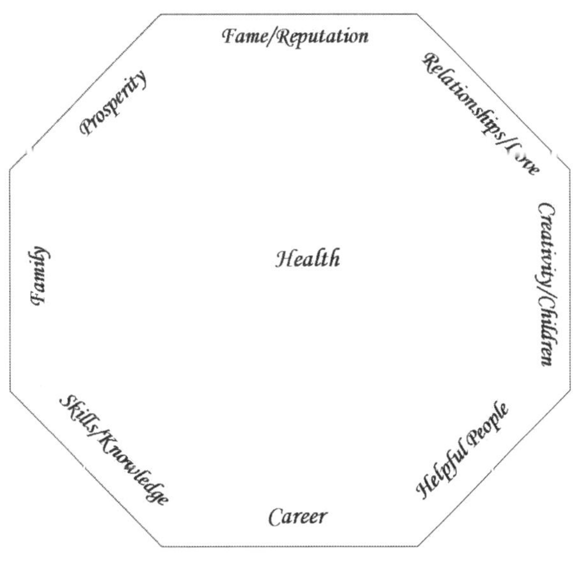

I am in no way a feng shui expert, so I will not go into the nitty gritty of how to use this bagua, but I'll just give you some basics. Essentially, you can place the bagua over a blueprint of the main floor of your home or you can also place it over the layout of your office (or any individual room in your home). For our purposes, I will explain how it specifically works for your office.

When you are standing at the main entrance of the office looking into the room, you are standing somewhere in the bottom of the bagua, either in the *skills and knowledge*, *career*, or *helpful people* guas. For example, if the door is in the center of the wall, the entrance is in *career* or if the door is in the right corner of the wall as you are looking into the office, the entrance is in *helpful people.* So as you look into your office, the farthest left hand corner from the entrance is the *prosperity* corner. The center of the back wall farthest away from the entrance is the *fame and reputation* area. The farthest right hand corner from the entrance is the *relationships and love* corner. Just go around the room to find the different guas. If you place the bagua over the blueprint of your home, it works the same way – your main entrance is in one of the three bottom guas, the farthest right corner of your home is the *prosperity* gua, etc.

Each gua has specific auspicious colors associated with it (i.e., the *prosperity* color is purple, the *fame* color is red, etc.) as well as having natural elements associated with it like fire, water, wood, earth, and metal (i.e., the *fame* element is fire and the *career* element is water). So, if you want to enhance any particular areas of your life, you would enhance those areas (or guas) of your home or office by adding auspicious colors and objects to the appropriate areas and removing inauspicious ones.

You may be completely confused by all of this, but if you want to read more, my favorite feng shui books are Move Your Stuff, Change Your Life by Karen Rauch Carter and Feng Shui Your Life by Jayme Barrett. Both of these books are easily accessible for feng shui novices. You don't have to "study" feng shui to get benefits from it. But if nothing else, removing your clutter, moving your desk and freeing your door will get the ch'i moving in the right direction!

The Action Plans

We have now finished all the hard core explanations pertaining to most every aspect of your office. It is now time to get busy! There are two actions plans in this section – a quick fix and an intense overhaul. You can choose to do both, just one, or pick out a few tasks from each. Whatever you choose, I will warn you – organization is contagious!! You just might "get the fever!"

10 Things you can do RIGHT NOW to get organized

Here is a list of 10 things that address some of the major clutter factors. Some I have already mentioned in previous chapters and some are new. Some of these tasks could take a few minutes to complete and some might take a little planning and a few hours. If accomplishing the tasks on this list is the only thing you do from this book, you will be pleasantly surprised at what a difference it can make!

1. **Say goodbye to Post-It® Notes and Scrap Paper!** Are you addicted to tiny pieces of paper, some of them sticky and some of them not, that you can grab easily and write down someone's phone number, or a reminder, or a shopping list? Well, get over it! Talk about an unbelievable amount of clutter, besides the fact that it is a completely inefficient system. When was the last time you had to call someone and found yourself going crazy looking for that little pink Post-It® that you could have sworn was stuck to your desk? The solution to this problem is a simple one and something that I got from a few different Directors.

    - Purchase 12 One Subject spiral bound notebooks – one for each month of the year.
    - Keep one notebook on your desk at all times.
    - At the start of each day write the date on one page in the notebook and use this exclusively for all of your immediate "jot down" needs – phone

numbers, to do lists, instant ideas, etc. Each day gets a new set of pages with the date on it. This notebook is your Daily Phone Journal.

Your Daily Phone Journal can go with you, if needed, but make sure it is located on your desk when you are in your office. This way you will be able to keep track of all of your notes, numbers and stuff and eliminate all of that scrap paper clutter

- Right now, gather every scrap piece a paper and hanging Post-It® note and transfer all the information that you want to keep into your first notebook. You'll probably find that you can throw out many of those papers without transferring anything!

2. **Accept the fact that your wall is not a bulletin board!** Just because you can pin things on your wall, doesn't mean you should. I know...you are saying, "But I'm a visual person. I have to have visual aids in front of me." I understand that perfectly. I know how important a goal poster and unit tracking chart is. However, if every inch of your wall is covered with posters and charts and sayings and tracking sheets, not to mention calendars, commission statements, receipts, newsletters and phone numbers (written on Post-It® notes!) then it's just too much. With all of those things in front of you, you are visually over-stimulated. You can't really be motivated by any of them because you can't focus your full attention on any of them.

   The only things that should be on your wall are things that inspire and motivate you – I don't need to list the things that are appropriate because you alone know what motivates you. However, you really have to look at everything in front of you and ask yourself these questions:

a) Does this motivate me to work?
b) Does this inspire me to feel better about myself?
c) Is this going to help me achieve my goals?

- Find a way to combine visual aids so that you have less on your wall, but you are still able to have all the tracking you need. Instead of having a Star Consultant Tracker, a Career Path Unit Tracker and a Production Tracker, find a way to combine all of these, so that all of the information is in one dynamic visual aid.
- I've had a Director suggest that you have a bulletin board with a white board on one side and cork on the other. This way, you can write current ideas and goals or top consultants that you want to focus on directly on the white board. Just make sure that you treat your white board as a piece of art. Make it legible and inspirational and update it often.
- Use your actual (reasonably sized) bulletin board as your goal poster. Post the pictures of the Cadillac, your head fused on a National Sales Director Suit, pictures of the location of the Top Director Trip and whatever else you are working towards. This is a great self-contained canvas that can display this all important tool. All of the other kinds of things that typically go on a bulletin board like phone numbers, documents, reminder notices and the like should be put in your In/Out File System (see *The Secret to a Clutter Free Office – The In/Out File System* Chapter for more details) and taken care of in a timely manner. Having them in front of you creating visual clutter does nothing to inspire you. If you are faithful to your In/Out File System, then you don't need all of those miscellaneous items hanging on the wall.

- The time has come...take everything off your wall. Ask yourself the three questions listed above about each item. Then decide if it must be on your wall. Can it be filed? Can it be thrown out? Can it be given away?
- Once you've decided what you must have on your wall, design it like you are putting art on your wall. Choose one or two special areas where you will display your visuals. Make it creative, artistic and beautiful.

3. **Purge the chatchkas – NOW!** I remember that one of the first things my Adoptee Director told me was that Mary Kay people are very prize-oriented. Oh yes, indeed-y! I got sucked in – the pins, rings, necklaces, bags, desk accessories, plaques, frames – the list goes on and on. The problem is that all that stuff adds up. Now, I'm not saying that the bumble bee paper weight, the beautifully framed picture of Mary Kay, the silver wings plaque and the crystal swan are bad to have around you. However, if it were just those four little items, there wouldn't be a problem, would there? I've been in the business for a relatively short period of time and I've accumulated an unbelievable amount of stuff. For those of you who have been in this business for 10, 15, or 20 years, the "stuff" list is endless – not only the things we receive as gifts, but the things we buy! How much money did you spend at the concession booth at Seminar this past year? Again, the only things that should be visible in your office are the things that motivate and inspire you. All the others should be given away or thrown out.

    - Look at every chatchka you have on your desk, on top of your cabinets, in your book shelves, on your wall and ask yourself the three questions:

        a) Does this motivate me to work?
        b) Does this inspire me to feel better about myself?

c) Is this going to help me achieve my goals?

- Decide what you want to do with the ones that don't fit those three questions. You can give them away to your consultants or offspring Directors. You can donate them to the Salvation Army or Goodwill. Or you can throw them out.

Something else that needs to be addressed here are pictures. I know you are thinking, "Don't you dare touch my pictures!" However, there are a couple of problems here. First of all, I have nothing against pictures of your family members, your unit members, your next door neighbors...but again do these pictures inspire and motivate you to work and succeed? If they do, fine. Keep them. If they don't, find a place in your home where they would be enjoyed by everyone. But if you do decide to keep them, display only the ones that inspire you, placing them in a special place where they will be respected. If you put 20 framed pictures on top of a cabinet, you can't enjoy them, nor can you give each picture the respect it deserves. All you see is more clutter. Choose the ones that are most important to you and find a new home for the rest.

Remember that the stuff does not represent the person who gave it to you. Stuff is just stuff. What is important is the memory of that person or event and memories don't leave clutter.

4. **Do away with Stackable Trays and Paper Sorters!** I've said it before, but I'll say it again – I HATE stackable trays and paper sorters. These items are nothing but collectors of stuff and dust that very rarely get cleaned out. They also take up a great deal of space on your desk and are generally unattractive. The answer to this problem is the In/Out File System. It is a very specific hanging file system that allows you to temporarily rid your desk of all the paper it collects and because each file

is specific to an aspect of your daily, weekly, or monthly business, the files get cleaned out on a regular basis.

- Purchase a desktop hanging file system, about 12 hanging file folders, and Smead Viewables® hanging file folder tabs. Create these files:
  - *a) Director* **(your name) TO DO** – put the label on the far left of the folder
  - **b) Assistant TO DO** – put the label on the far right of the folder
  - **c) Accounts Receivable** – put this label and all the rest of the labels below in the center on the file folder (5 slots from either side)
  - **d) Customer Sales**
  - **e) Customer Returns**
  - **f) Inventory Orders**
  - **g) Loan/Borrow/Personal Use**
  - **h) New Consultants**
  - **i) Newsletter**
  - **j) Receipts**
  - **k) To File**
  - **l) Unit Meeting**

Read *The Secret to a Clutter Free Office – The In / Out File System* Chapter to learn how to use each of these files, if you have not done so already.

5. **Understand that the top of your desk is not a supply closet!** Yes, you need pens, scissors, tape, paper clips, staples, labels, and numerous other "supplies." However, these items need not be all on your desk. These are the only items that should be on your desk:

- Telephone and answering machine (if you don't have voicemail, which I suggest you eventually get)
- Calculator
- Rolodex (if you have one)

- Pencil cup with a few good pens and pencils, 1 pair of scissors and a letter opener (optional)
- Your datebook (or PDA) and your Daily Phone Journal

That's it! All the rest of the supplies should be in a drawer. If you don't have a desk drawer (although, think about getting a desk that does have a drawer, if possible), then get a small desk supply drawer bin at your favorite office supply store. You should store any bulk supplies in large plastic drawer bins, either in a closet or under your desk or in another part of the office. These bins can be purchased almost anywhere – office, linen or kitchen supply stores.

- Clean off the top of your desk right now. So you may be thinking, "Where do I put all the stuff?" Well, I am assuming you have already created your In/Out File System. If not, now is the time to do it. That system is the answer to having a place for everything.
- Remember that you also need to address the chatchka situation. Just like when you are deciding what to hang on your wall, look at every little knick-knack that is currently sitting on your desk and ask yourself the three questions.
- You may also need to clean out your desk drawers, so you can put in the stuff that is no longer going on your desk. Again, use your purging techniques – when was the last time you used this? Is this still usable? Can this be filed or stored elsewhere?

6. **Do not keep business cards!** How many business cards do you come home with from any given Company event - Directors, Consultants, and others? These little pieces of cardstock accumulate and, more often than not, get thrown on the desk or in your briefcase, never to be seen again. The rule is: enter the information into your address book (electronic or not) or rolodex immediately when you get home and then throw the card out. If you

use an online address book, you can usually categorize your contacts into Business or Personal; some of them even allow you to categorize your contacts further into Consultants, Directors, Vendors, etc. Whatever your system is, use it faithfully! You won't believe how much clutter this little step will eliminate.

- Find every business card hiding on your desk, in your desk, in your briefcase, on your bulletin board, or under your desk blotter. Look through them, throwing away any you know you will never need. Enter the information from the rest into your favorite address book and throw them out when you are finished.

7. **Vow to no longer be a bag lady!** I totally admit it. I am a sucker for bags myself! I purchase purses and bags at least 3 to 4 times a year and the old bags fall by the wayside even though they are still perfectly good; not to mention the fact that they all cost me money! I don't know one Mary Kay Director who does not have a pile of bags. You get new ones at every Career Conference and Seminar – the company ones, as well as the cheap ones that are sold by the miscellaneous vendors at these events. There are, of course, the more expensive briefcases and shoulder bags that we purchase at the mall. But regardless of where you got them, this is the deal...you really don't need them all! No really.....you DON'T need them all.

    - Decide what you need your bags for. When I say *need*, I mean NEED. There are plenty of bags you might like or want, but the issue here is efficiency. You need a separate bag for each event, such as: selling appointments, unit meetings, recruiting interviews, and company events. Decide what bags you really need and then choose the best bags that will fill those needs.
    - If your bags are in good shape, give them away – to Goodwill or offer a promotion, giving them

away to your consultants. If your bags have seen better days, throw them out!

8. **Realize that, just because you don't see clutter in your computer, it's still there!** How many e-mails did you get today? If you are included in some Top Director's address books, chances are you received upwards to 20 or 30 e-mails today alone. Sometimes you read these e-mails and sometimes you don't. Either way, your inbox gets inundated with mail. That mail takes up valuable space on your hard drive (the storage part of your computer) and should be eliminated when you are finished with it. When your hard drive gets full, your computer runs slower and can start having annoying little technical problems. It's time to do some computer cleanup and we're going to focus on the e-mail situation. If you decide to do the *Seven Step Action Plan* we will delve into the other areas of the computer then.

    - Let's start with the inbox. Glance through every e-mail (you don't necessarily have to read them all, you can tell what they are by their subject) and delete the ones you don't want. If there are ones that you want to save, create a folder in your mailbox where you can collect like items. For example, create a folder called *Selling ideas* and whenever you receive an e-mail from another Director with a great selling idea, drag that e-mail to this folder. You can create as many folders as you want, which acts as your online filing cabinet where you can find things easily. Contact your e-mail program administrator to figure out how to create a new folder if you don't know how.
    - Now let's move to your sent items box. Did you realize that every time you reply to an e-mail or send a new e-mail, a copy gets saved in your sent items box? Again, that is an enormous amount of mail that is taking up your hard drive space. You can delete every piece of e-mail in this box.

Left-click on the first e-mail in the list so that it is highlighted. Scroll down to the last e-mail in the list. Click and hold down the shift key on your keyboard and then while you are holding that down, *left*-click on the last e-mail message of the list. Now you will see that the entire list is highlighted. Hit the delete button on the keyboard and the computer will ask if you if you really want to move all these items to the trash. Click on *OK* and they should all disappear.

- Now your inbox is cleaned out and your sent items folder is empty and you feel refreshed and de-cluttered! But wait….it's not over! All of those items that you deleted were not actually taken off your computer. They were simply moved to the deleted items folder or trash can. So, you need to go to that deleted items folder or trash can and empty it. You can do that in the same way that you emptied the sent items folder, or your e-mail program might actually have an "empty the trash" button. Either way, make sure you don't leave this task without cleaning out that folder.

9. **Feng Shui the entrance to your office.** OK, now you think I've gone mad; especially if you haven't read the chapter on the benefits of feng shui. But seriously, this can make a huge difference in the productivity of your office. One of the principles of feng shui states that entrances into rooms should be clear and open. Your door should be able to open all the way and you should be able to walk a straight path into the room without obstruction. If the door is blocked partially, for instance, if there is a bookcase so close to the door that the door can't open all the way, then negative energy cannot flow out of the room and positive energy cannot flow into the room. You can also feel negative energy if you can't enter the room in a straight path. If your doorway is surrounded by "stuff" that requires you to jimmy yourself in on an angle,

chances are you've got bad ch'i. Now, I **know** you think I'm crazy.

- Look at the entrance to your office. Can the door open all the way? Is the space around the entrance clear or do you feel like you are packed like a sardine in that entrance? If the answer to either of these questions is, "No" then you need to do something about it. Remove anything that is hanging on the door. You should try to move the furniture so that the entrance is open and clear. Now, if you are saying, "There's no way I can move the furniture. My office is too small" then you seriously need to consider purging some furniture. Chances are, if you really start clearing the clutter (paper, old inventory, chatchkas, etc.), you won't need that extra piece of furniture anyway.

10. **Be faithful to just 10 minutes a day to clean off your desk!** If you start your day by walking into your office and looking at a desk that is piled high with papers, Post-Its®, and projects, chances are that you won't be as productive that day. Why? Because you will sit at your desk and wonder "Where do I start?" You'll spend too much time looking for things that you thought were *right here*. You will start on one thing, but the clutter distracts you, so you don't finish any one thing; you just move on to another. This is the problem with a messy desk. Conversely, when you walk into an office in the morning with no clutter on the desk, the possibilities are endless! You are able to be *proactive* by choosing your work that you will complete that day rather than *reactive* by the work (or clutter) choosing you.

    - If you have completed the previous nine tasks, congratulations!! You should now have a significantly improved office space. Now make the decision to commit 10 minutes every night to keeping it looking that way – starting tomorrow.

The Seven Step Action Plan

OK, you've read the book and you are inspired and fired up to completely organize your life! Or maybe you haven't read the book and you just want to get to it! Either way: Congratulations on making the decision to get organized. You will not regret any step of it.

This **Seven Step Action Plan** as laid out below is somewhat of a skeleton outline. There are things that I will tell you to do, but in order to do them correctly; I suggest you read the chapters on those particular areas in order to understand the specifics on how to actually complete the tasks.

I want to warn you that this action plan is pretty intense. Most of this plan is essentially what I do for my clients in about three 8 to 12 hour days. Remember that I'm a professional and I work very fast! It will probably take you longer than three days; however, you will see that I have marked out certain steps that can be easily delegated. You can have your assistant or reliable family members or neighbors do many of these jobs. Just make sure that you reward them and yourself when each step is completed! That will keep you motivated to continue.

You can decide if you want to do all of these steps or just a few. However, if you are really committed to getting organized and you are going to follow this action plan, look at this project as a Weekend Warrior project. If you decide to redecorate a room, you plan, prepare, and attack; finishing it in one fell swoop (or that is, at least, your intent). You can, of course, break these steps up and do one or more during 1 day a week or 1 day a month, but just as when you are in DIQ or achieving your other goals in Mary Kay, success is much easier when it is FAST! If you can find a way to schedule this project into as many consecutive days as possible, you will be focused and motivated to finish it. Chances are, if you start it on one day and then don't think about it for a week, you are never going to accomplish the goal.

So get ready, get set, get organized!

Step 1 - Plan it

This step must be done by you although you may enlist some help

It is very important that you fully complete this step. I know you are excited and want to dig in, but if you don't plan properly, chances are that you are going to get sidetracked.

- **Fill out a Weekly Plan Sheet for your organization project.** Look at the steps you want to complete this week and determine how long you may need to complete them. Be realistic and plan in some resting time. If you don't, you will easily become overwhelmed and want to give up.
- **Plan out the supplies you will need.** You will need plenty of trash bags for garbage, boxes for items you will be giving away, file folders, hanging files, Smead Viewables®, and so on.
- **Look at your furniture and decide if you need to change anything.** Do you need shelves, a new filing cabinet, a new chair, storage boxes for your small inventory items? Decide if that is in the budget and make a plan to purchase them and assemble them (if necessary) before you organize that particular area.
- **Decide if you really need all that furniture in your office.** Most often, when I am organizing an office, we do so much purging that we end up needing *less* in the way of shelves, drawers, or cabinets. If you already know that your office is way too full of furniture, remove it and when you are purging remember that you have less storage space. That will get you motivated to purge!
- **Plan your zones.** Where will your inventory zone, your skin care class zone, or your office supplies zone be? When you are organizing, you will want to make sure you are following your zoning plan.

Step 2 – Organize your Inventory

This step is easily delegated

I always start my organizing with this step because it is fairly quick and easy. If you are delegating this step, you can move on to another step while your assistant (or whomever) is doing this.

- **Put all of your inventory together in the inventory zone.** Find any "hidden" product; product that is in your car, or in another room, or still in Mary Kay shipping boxes.
- **Disassemble any baskets or displays that no longer fit easily in your office and add that product to the shelves.** The packaging from those baskets will now be stored in the packaging zone.
- **Purge your discontinued product and put it in a box to go out.** Make a plan to deliver this product to its new home within a few days.
- **Now that all the inventory is in the zone, organize it on the shelves in the same categories as the order sheet** - TimeWise, Basic Skin Care, Customized Skin Care, Fragrances, Body Care, Glamour, etc. Limited edition items can either stay separate or stored with their main categories like glamour or body care. If you want to, label all of the small compartments that you store your glamour in with the shade name so it is easily accessible.
- **Once all of your product is organized, do a complete inventory**. Count all of your full-size demo products as well as any product that is already packaged to sell (i.e., the products in a filled travel roll-up). Separate your inventory count into the following categories:

    - Product on the shelf or packaged to sell including any discontinued product that you intend to sell
    - Full-size product that you use for demo
    - Discontinued product that you are giving away

You are doing this inventory count so that when it is time to update your computer (Step 6) you have the most current count to enter. You need a record of the discontinued product for tax purposes and you need a record of the current demo products IF you haven't already made a record of them. You don't need to inventory samples – they are simply too difficult to keep track of. Place these inventory counts close to the computer when you are finished so they are easily found when you need to enter them in.

It is very important that, after you have taken inventory, you are very diligent about keeping record of any product that leaves your shelf or goes on your shelf between the time that you counted and the time you enter it into the computer. This count is your fresh start, so get into the habit of writing out sales tickets for everything that comes and goes.

Step 3 – Create your Books and Media, Packaging and Office Supplies Zones

This step is easily delegated

Read *The Art of Zoning – And you don't need a permit* and the *To Purge or Not to Purge – That is the Question* Chapters to find out more about this step.

- **Purge books, media, and office supplies** - old books, tapes, CDs, videos, old ribbon and wrapping paper, old printer paper, baskets, old pens and markers, etc. Either throw them out or put them in a box to give away.
- **Purge your chatchkas.** Remember that you only want to keep and display the things that inspire and motivate you. All the rest can be given away to make someone else's life happy.
- **Organize your bookshelves.** Try organizing them using the third, third, third method. One third of the shelves should be filled with books, one third should be decorative with your chatchkas or pictures, and one

third should be empty space. This is the most pleasing way to fill your shelves. They don't look cluttered and you can find things easily. If you can't do this because of the stuff to space ratio, make sure they are as organized as possible.

- **Organize your books and media in like categories.** Your books can be separated into Director's Manuals, Consultant Manuals, MK Autobiography's, Business Success, Personal Success, etc. Your media should be organized into Recruiting, Product Information, Inspiration, etc. To organize your media, videos can stand or stack on shelves, and you can use square baskets or decorative boxes for tapes and CDs.
- **Set up your office supply zone by using plastic storage drawers or shelves in a closet or whatever you find most convenient.** Put smaller items like staples and paper clips and the like in a basket in this area.
- **Set up your packaging zone in the same way.** Put like items together in drawers or boxes and put them in your closet or on shelves.
- **Set up your mailing supplies zone.** All of your padded envelopes, packing tape, return address labels, etc. belong in this area.

Step 4 – Purge your Files and Create a File System

This step must be done by you

This is the only step that I make my clients do. Of course, I give them advice if they need it, but when it comes to purging paper and creating a file system, it is important that they know what they have, as well as how and where it will be filed. Otherwise, you won't be able to find anything once you are organized. I will also warn you that this is definitely the most annoying step. It may be hard to get through, so give yourself a lot of breaks! Again, this is just an outline of this step. Make sure you read the *Papers! Papers! Or The Joy of Filing* Chapter to get all the nitty gritty about how to purge and create a file system.

- **Begin the initial sort.** Take all papers (big and small) off from the desk, out from under the desk, out of the filing cabinets and off from your wall, putting it all in the center of the room along with a large garbage can.
    - In the initial sort make four piles - company literature, personal business, training, and one for stuff that doesn't belong in the office (taxes, house bills that you don't pay, spouses or children's papers that don't have anything to do with your business).
    - The first three piles will all be put in three separate filing drawers.
    - In this initial sort don't take a lot of time to read through everything. You are just separating like papers. Anything you know immediately when you touch it that you can throw out, do it.
- **Then begin the scrutinized organization.** This is where you go through each paper in your piles; throw out what you don't need and create file categories that will become the titles of your new file folders. Make sure you don't over-categorize - put like things together in one folder (see the *Papers! Papers! Or The Joy of Filing* Chapter for specifics).
- **Write the name of the file on the pile on a Post-It®** after you have completed separating all the file categories. Then stack them in alphabetical order.
- **Type up the labels and put them in the appropriate drawers (in alphabetical order).**
- **Make a pile of all those little scrap pieces of paper and business cards.** When you are done with your file system, transfer the information you want to keep from these small papers into your notebook or rolodex and throw the papers out.

Step 5 – Organize your Desk and your Wall

This step should be done by you but portions of it can be delegated

- **Go through drawers, look at the top of your desk and purge** - old pens, old supplies, garbage, chatchkas - keep only a small collection of supplies that you need; the rest should be in your office supply zone. Other things that can go inside your desk include postcards and stationery. Again, don't keep every postcard and every flowered piece of paper in here. If you don't have the room inside your desk, find a decorative photo box to put them in and place it near or under your desk.
- **Completely clean off the top of the desk so that it is bare!** Then, only put the allowed items back on the desk (see *The Art of Zoning – And you Don't Need a Permit* Chapter for the approved list).
- **Get a 3-ring binder and index tabs and set up your focus folder.** Categories in the folder can be:

    - Consultant List
    - New Consultants
    - On Target Stars, Recruiters, etc.
    - Monthly Production Projection
    - Goals
    - Top Consultants (Stars, Super Stars)
    - Calendar (Weekly Plan Sheet)

  You can obviously come up with more categories that are important to you.
- **Take this time to set up a Daily Phone Journal** that you keep on your desk to replace all those scrap papers.
- **Clean everything off your walls and redecorate.** Make some serious decisions about what is important enough for you to keep on your walls. Create organized tracking charts and creative goal posters, if you want. Decide what pictures are important enough for you to display, but remember, the only things that should be on your wall are things that motivate and inspire you. Do not use your wall as a catch-all.
- **Create the In/Out File system.** See *The Secret to a Paperless Office – The In/Out File System* Chapter for instructions.

Step 6 – Complete your Computer data entry

This step can easily be delegated

This is another tedious step; however, this is easily delegated to someone else. This is the step that gets your computer system organized by entering all of your important business information and cleaning out unnecessary files.

- **Update (or create) your Boulevard® software.** If you are not familiar with Boulevard®, read the documentation or watch the DVD training that comes with the program. Call technical support when you get stuck. They are very friendly! Make sure to cover the following:
    - Enter all of your customer profiles and include a record of their past product purchases if you desire. When you are finished, you can throw the paper profiles out.
    - Import your production from Desktop Office Manager® into Boulevard® which should import all of your unit members' information. You may need to update the information, entering past production if you want to keep a record or other personal information such as e-mail addresses and birthdays.
    - Enter any outstanding Loan/Borrow items
    - Enter inventory count (from Step 2) as a new order. IMPORTANT: Do this as the last step of your Boulevard® data entry. This way, if you enter any products in loan/borrow or individual customers, it will not get counted against your inventory.
- **Update your group e-mail addresses**. Make sure your current working unit members are included and the non-workers are not. Make sure all the e-mail addresses for your unit members are wo rking. Have your assistant call everyone to make sure.
- **Go through your inbox and save any e-mails in document form to keep and throw out the rest** - delete the items in the trash box and delete messages

in the sent items box. (See *Your Computer – Friend or Foe?* Chapter for more instructions on this)

- **Organize all of your Mary Kay documents in the computer.** File them in new categorized folders just like you did in your filing cabinet near your desk. Again, like documents should go together with an easy to remember title.
- **Finally, do your computer maintenance**.
    - o Defragment (or optimize) your hard drive
    - o Remove any programs that you are not using from your hard drive
    - o Clean out the temporary internet files and cookies
    - o Do a Spybot Search and Destroy check.

Full instructions on how to do these tasks are in the *Your Computer – Friend or Foe?* Chapter.

Step 7 – Create your Mission Statement and Realize your Dreams

This step must be done by you

This is the day that you sit at your clean desk and look out at your completely organized and uncluttered office and you focus on why you did all of this. It is time that you seriously think about your values and your dreams and you write them into your mission statement. You can simply sit down and write, or, if you don't know where to start and you need guidance, go to the Franklin Covey site (http://www.franklincovey.com/missionbuilder/index.html). Once you've finished your mission statement, make sure you share it with your family. And then you should make a family mission statement together.

Live your life by your mission and your business will explode with positive results. But that is not the only thing that matters. What matters most is....well, only you can answer that question. The tools that I have given you in this book are only a vehicle to clear the way for you to achieve the best you have to offer. Now that you are free, finally free to succeed, go out and make the world a better place!

Epilogue

So if you've read the entire book, you may be completely overwhelmed with all the detailed information I have provided. You may know that you need to get organized and you may want to get organized, but it seems like too much of a daunting task.

By now, you must know that I fully believe that if you take that step and remove the clutter from your life, you will be able to achieve your goals much faster and easier than ever before. So I want to encourage you not to be afraid and if you can't foresee doing this on your own, seek professional help!

There is an organization called NAPO – The National Association of Professional Organizers (www.napo.com). If you visit their website, you can search for a professional organizer in your area. They will not necessarily know the Mary Kay business, but they can certainly help you remove all your unnecessary clutter.

Or you can check out my website and see the services I offer (www.reginazona-mkorganizer.com). I work only with Mary Kay Directors and Consultants. I am available for personal organizing in New England and I can also do phone consultations off-site for those of you in other parts of the country that would like some guidance. Please visit my website for more information. You will also find my e-mail address and phone number there.

You may think you can't afford to hire someone to come in and sort through your stuff. But I ask you this: if you are not where you want to be in your business and your life, can you afford NOT to get someone's help? Trust me, it just might be the most important thing you do.

Appendices

Websites I recommend

Organizational System Solutions (MY website)

www.reginazona-mkorganizer.com
I would be lying if I said that this were not my favorite website! Check out information on all the services I offer, workshops I teach and how to contact me personally.

Mary Kay Services and Software

Main Street Software
www.mainstsoftware.com
This is where you can purchase the Boulevard® program.

Unit News
www.unitnews.com
This is an excellent and inexpensive way to delegate your monthly newsletter creation.

Unit Net
www.unitnet.com
You probably know about this site, but if you don't, check it out. Directors from Nationals on down have personal websites that you can access. You can also sign up for your own website for as little as $15 a month. It's an excellent way to communicate with your unit and sister Directors. Just make sure you update your site on a regular basis!

Free Software Downloads

Adobe Acrobat Reader®
http://www.adobe.com/products/acrobat/readstep2.html
This is the program that allows you to read PDF files.

PDF995® PDF Creator and Printer Driver
http://www.pdf995.com/download.html

This is the program which allow you convert any Word or Publisher document into a PDF. Make sure you download both the Converter and the Printer Driver and read the directions on how to use them.

SpyBot Search and Destroy®
http://download.com.com/3000-8022-10122137.html
This program will destroy any SpyWare on your computer.

STOPzilla
www.stopzilla.com
This program got the highest marks for effective Pop-Up blocking.

SAproxy-Pro
http://downloads-zdnet.com.com/SAproxy-Pro/3000-2382-10298204.html
This program with help you control all of those spam e-mails. It is free for the first thirty days and then will cost you $30.

Organizational websites

Get Organized Now
www.getorganizednow.com
This is a website by personal organizer Maria Gracia which is chock full of information on how to organize every corner of your house and more. You can also sign up for a weekly newsletter that will be e-mailed to you with lots of great tips.

National Association of Professional Organizers
www.napo.com
This is where you can find a professional organizer in your area.

Office Supplies and Stationery

Staples
www.staples.com
The thing I love about Staples online is they offer free delivery on any order over $50 and it will usually arrive at your home the next business day. This is where you can get anything (even furniture) and my favorite Smead Viewables®.

Buy Online Now
www.buyonlinenow.com
The office supply store has great prices and they have everything.

Paper Direct
www.paperdirect.com
They have wonderful stationery in every form you can think of. They can be a little pricey but if you want to make an impact with your image on paper, you should check it out.

Organizational tools

Get Organized Company
www.getorganizedco.com
This is where you can find the storage boxes for your inventory. They are relatively inexpensive and enormously efficient!

Stack and Stacks
www.stackandstacks.com
This place is an organizer's dream. Every kind of container you can think of (and more) is for sale.

Organize Everything
http://store.yahoo.com/organizeeverything1/index.html
Another great website for all the fun organizational tools you could ever need.

Business and Life Guidance

Franklin Covey

www.franklincovey.com
This is where you can purchase all of Stephen Covey's books including The 7 Habits of Highly Effective People and time management tools like planners, binders and PDAs. You can also find information on how to locate a personal coach.

Franklin Covey Mission Statement Builder

http://www.franklincovey.com/missionbuilder/index.html
They will guide you through a series of questions to discover your values and write your Mission Statement. When you are finished, they e-mail you a copy of it.

Feng Shui

Feng Shui Palace

www.fengshuipalace.com
This is Karen Rauch Carter's site, the author of Move your Stuff, Change your Life. She has really nice charts of the Bagua with full explanations of how they can help you.

Great Books I highly recommend

Some of these books I referenced in various chapters. Others are just great books that I think you should read.

Organizational Books

Organizing from the Inside Out by Julie Morgenstern
Henry Holt and Co. LLC, 1998

Organizing for Dummies by Eileen Roth and Elizabeth Miles
Hungry Minds, 2001

Cut the Clutter and Stow the Stuff by Lori Baird, ed.
Yankee Publishing, Inc., 2002

How to Get Organized When you Don't Have the Time by Stephanie Culp
Writer's Digest Books, 1986

Time Management Books

Time Management from the Inside Out by Julie Morgenstern

Henry Holt and Co., LLC, 2000

Time Management for the Creative Person by Lee Silber
Three Rivers Press, 1998

Business and Life Management

The 7 Habits of Highly Effective People by Stephen R. Covey
Fireside, 1990

Coach Yourself to Success by Talane Miedaner
Contemporary Books, 2000

Feel the Fear and Do it Anyway by Susan Jeffers
Ballantine Books, 1987

Who Moved My Cheese by Spencer Johnson, M.D.
G.P. Putnam's Sons, 1998

Financial Success

Smart Couples Finish Rich by David Bach
Broadway Books, 2002

Feng Shui

Move your Stuff, Change your Life by Karen Rauch Carter
Fireside, 2000

Feng Shui your Life by Jayme Barrett
Sterling Publishing Co., Inc., 2003

The Western Guide to Feng Shui by Terah Kathryn Collins
Hay House, Inc., 1996

Office Feng Shui by Darrin Zeer
Chronicle Books LLC, 2004

Endnotes

1 On Purpose Associates, “Right Brain vs. Left Brain.” Funderstanding, Engaging Kids, 25 June 2004 <http://www.funderstanding.com/right_left_brain.cfm>.

2 Julie Morgenstern, Organizing From The Inside Out (New York: Henry Holt and Company, LLC, 1998) 17.

3 Morgenstern.

4 Morgenstern.

5 Morgenstern 15.

6 Main Street Software, Inc., “Boulevard®.” Boulevard®, Home Page, 7 July 2004 <http://www.mainstsoftware.com>.

7 Robert Vamosi, “Stop direct marketers from spying on you.” ZDNet, Product Reviews, 17 May 2004, 7 July 2004 <http://reviews-zdnet.com.com/Spyware/4520-3513_16-5134965-1.html?tag=prmo1>.

8 Stephen R. Covey, The 7 Habits of Highly Effective People (New York: Fireside, 1989) 129.

9 Stephen R. Covey, The 7 Habits of Highly Effective People: Personal Coaching System (USA: Franklin Covey Co., 2000) “Habit 2”, 3.

10 Covey, The 7 Habits of Highly Effective People 106.

11 Covey, The 7 Habits of Highly Effective People 145.

About the Author

REGINA ZONA is founder of Organizational System Solutions, a personal organizing company exclusively for Mary Kay Directors and Consultants. She not only addresses the physical clutter and organizational details that plague the lives of her clients but also creates systems that allow her clients to get out of the office and achieve their highest goals. She has organized the offices and lives of Mary Kay women at all levels, from NIQ to DIQ and is a Mary Kay recruiter herself. Regina is also an acclaimed opera singer and has sung all over the world in such places as Germany, Japan, Mexico, and several cities in the US. She currently lives in Milford, CT.